KiDS

DoGS

FUN

KiDS

+

DoGS

=

FUN

Great Activities Your Kids and Dogs
Can Do Together

Jacqueline O'Neil

HOWELL
BOOK
HOUSE

Howell Book House
Macmillan General Reference
A Simon & Schuster Macmillan Company
1633 Broadway
New York, NY 10019

MACMILLAN is a registered trademark of Macmillan, Inc.

Library of Congress Cataloging-in-Publication Data

O'Neil, Jacqueline.
Kids + dogs = fun : great activities your kids and dogs can do
    together / Jacqueline O'Neil.
            p.   cm.
    ISBN 0-87605-754-7
    1. Dog sports.   2. Dogs—Training.   3. Dogs—Social aspects.
4. Children and animals.   I. Title.
SF424.054   1996
636.7'088—dc20   96-29223
                                                   CIP

Book design by Scott Meola

Manufactured in the United States of America
10 9 8 7 6 5 4 3 2 1

To my mother, Dori Freedman, and her husband, Needham Parrish: because the word "fun" always makes me think of you.

Part III: Staying Motivated

INTRODUCTION

Dear Parent,

Welcome to the wonderful world of kids and dogs—an awesome place, full of exciting events, rewarding activities, and wholesome young people. In this world, peer pressure pushes youngsters toward acting responsibly and achieving their goals. In this world, teenagers and their parents have satisfying conversations and exchange ideas. In this world, shy children slowly blossom, sullen children smile as they feel the first flush of success, and careless youngsters take pride in their emerging sense of responsibility.

If your child is dog-crazy, count it as a blessing. Kids deeply involved in productive hobbies are happier and healthier than their bored counterparts. They are also wiser. The attributes kids learn while doing dog sports, such as patience and prioritizing goals, serve them well throughout their lives.

If your child has been begging for a dog, or already has one and wants to learn how to train it, this book will tell you how to get started. Part I gives you general information—the whats, whys, and hows of dog sports, and parenting kids who participate in them. It includes quizzes to help you decide if your child is ready to be a dog owner, if your dog is a suitable candidate for training, and which activities are most appropriate for both of them.

Part II highlights a baker's dozen of productive activities that kids and dogs enjoy together. Each chapter is designed to give you the feel of the activity and answer your whats—what it's like to participate, what it takes to succeed, what your child will learn, and what your role will be. The first eight activities are available to dogs of all shapes and sizes, purebred or mixed. The latter five ventures are available only to purebred registered dogs, and four of those showcase the inherited instincts of certain breeds.

Part III is the section to turn to for extra motivation. It begins with a chapter on keeping the good times going, and includes information on related organizations and recommended reading. These will come in handy if you want to explore the activities in more detail or find like-minded individuals to work with.

I like books that quote experts, so I interviewed several of the most knowledgeable people in the field and quoted them liberally. In fact, I'm proud to say that no one knows more about the child-dog relationship than the experts in this book. That's because most of them are either the parents of dog-crazy kids or the kids themselves. The exceptions are a child psychologist, a dog training instructor of renown, and several 4-H leaders. I thank all these experts for their insightful opinions.

If I were reading this book, I'd wonder how the author managed to find and quote so many terrific children. Did she survey organizations for award winners? Did she read a who's who of American youth? The answer is no. I didn't even look for outstanding children. To find kids involved in dog activities, I wrote letters to the editors of a few dog publications requesting that young people who participate in dog events contact me about appearing in a book. When kids responded, I asked for details about their dog endeavors, both positive and negative, and also aimed a few questions at their parents. Every child who answered my original request has been incorporated into this book. Not one was left out. So no, these young people weren't handpicked—and yes, they certainly are extraordinary.

When I started this book I knew that dogs and dog events were good for kids. Since learning more about these children, I'm especially excited about introducing you to their world. Welcome to the fun, the excitement, the sensitivity, the busy schedules, and the hard, satisfying work. Welcome to the wonderful world of kids and dogs.

Jacqueline O'Neil

Part 1

Chapter 1

Activities for Children and Their Dogs

Children and dogs participate together in over a dozen lively activities, some with several variations. Although not every activity is appropriate for every child or every dog, several choices are well suited to all child-and-dog teams.

This is Dustin Peterson with his Shetland Sheepdog, Nic-Nac Paddywack, CD, CGC. Dustin calls her Nikki. The "CD" stands for "Companion Dog," and means Nikki earned an obedience degree. Nikki is also a Canine Good Citizen (CGC).

ACTIVITIES FOR ALL DOGS

All dogs (purebred or mixed) can participate in 4-H dog projects, the American Kennel Club (AKC) Canine Good Citizen program, obedience and junior showmanship competition, agility trials, and tracking tests. Also, all gentle pets with the required training are welcome in animal-assisted therapy. Therapy dogs and their owners spread cheer by visiting nursing homes and other institutions.

ACTIVITIES FOR REGISTERED DOGS AND SPECIFIC BREEDS

Many activities for registered purebred dogs are breed specific, testing the dog's ability to perform the job for which it was originally bred. There are noncompetitive hunting tests for retrievers, spaniels, and pointing dogs. All of the traditional herding breeds may participate in herding tests and trials. Lure coursing events challenge the fleet-footed sighthounds, and earthdog tests are open to Dachshunds and the small terriers originally used as vermin hunters. In addition, all registered purebred dogs (that meet the requirements) may compete in the colorful canine version of beauty contests known as dog shows. So, whether Peggy and Kevin enjoy indoor or outdoor events, want to go hunting or help the handicapped, opportunities abound in the wonderful world of children and dogs.

Kids can get involved in all kinds of activities with their dogs. This girl and her dog are practicing one of the obstacles on an agility course.

ONE-SHOT DEALS AND PROGRESSIVE PROJECTS

Many children try a variety of activities until they find one captivating enough to hold their interest for a long time. This is good, because experimenting with a wide range of hobbies helps youngsters discover their own talents and leads to greater self-understanding. Yet it can be a difficult time for parents. Expenditures of money and time are involved when Kevin's early interest in the guitar gives way to skateboarding, and when Peggy switches from piano to ballet, and from ballet to gymnastics. So what should you do when Peggy tells you her ultimate hobby was waiting patiently by her feet all along—she wants to train Rex, the family dog? Or, Kevin wants a dog, and yes, he will take charge of the care and training.

A dog is a family member with feelings, not a disposable object to be discarded when the newness wears off, so carefully assess Kevin's commitment when he begs for a dog. Is it a sudden whim, or has he been "talking dog" for a long time? Has he studied different breeds so that he has a particular type of dog in mind? Does he mention training, 4-H projects, or dog care? If he has any other pets, is he responsible about them? These, and the questions found in the test in chapter 3, should help you decide if Kevin is ready for his own dog.

The good news is most dog sports have two things in common that let parents test the waters without immediately plunging into the deep end. That means if you already have a dog, and Peggy simply wants to learn how to train it for competitive events, your decision is not so momentous.

First of all, most dog sports feature a practical and achievable, yet challenging goal for novice trainers; one that usually includes earning ribbons or a certificate, and possibly even a permanent title for the dog. This makes it possible for parents to be supportive while waiting to see if Peggy will become bored before reaching her goal—or succeed and reap the rewards of a job well done.

Many children who achieve their goal consider it just the first step toward amplifying their training skills and attaining more advanced goals. And that leads to the second thing dog activities have in common. Most of them award honors at several progressive levels, so if Peggy and Kevin become captivated by the dog hobby, they can enjoy mastering more intricate skills for many years. In fact, working with dogs sometimes becomes a lifelong avocation.

DEGREES OF COMPETITION

In dog sports, a few activities are completely competitive, others are a combination of competitive and noncompetitive (allowing handlers the freedom to set and achieve their own personal goals), and some are incredibly rewarding without being competitive at all.

Dog shows and junior showmanship are strictly competitive. Dogs have to defeat other dogs in conformation (appearance) to win at dog shows, and handlers have to defeat other handlers to win junior showmanship.

Obedience is an example of a program that may be noncompetitive or extremely competitive, depending upon the handler's goal. On the noncompetitive side, Rex will receive a leg toward a title every time he earns a qualifying score. When he qualifies three times under three different judges, he will be awarded an official title and an attractive certificate. On the competitive side, awards from first through fourth place are presented to the top four qualifying dogs.

Other programs that award noncompetitive titles for achieving qualifying scores are hunting tests, earthdog tests, tracking, herding, lure coursing, and agility. While the first three operate solely as pass or fail tests, the latter three can be noncompetitive, or as competitive as Kevin and Peggy please.

No scores are awarded for participating in animal-assisted therapy or for raising a puppy as a service dog, but many believe these programs offer the greatest rewards of all.

AGE LIMITS

With the exception of junior showmanship, which is limited to youths under 18, Peggy and Kevin can continue their favorite dog activities all their lives. Competitive and noncompetitive programs both offer enough test levels and titles to keep them busy polishing their training and handling skills. And, as they become expert in their field, they may be invited to officiate or judge.

EXPENSES

Besides the regular expenses of owning a dog, such as food, toys, and health care, expect to pay for lessons, practice sessions (if applicable to the sport), club membership, special equipment, and entry fees for tests, trials, and shows. Expenses also include time and travel to lessons, meetings, practices, special events, and competitions.

TRAVEL

The distance you will travel to dog events depends on where you live and Peggy and Kevin's chosen activities. 4-H kids seldom have to travel far, unless they win at the county level and become eligible to

Kids can choose competitive or noncompetitive activities. Either way, the bonds they develop with their dogs will be strong ones. This is Marnie Kunz and Spanky.

compete at the state fair. But competing or testing to put titles on dogs often takes quite a bit of travel. Many events where points or legs toward titles are awarded are held in pairs, one on Saturday and another on Sunday (with different judges). When traveling a long distance, it pays to participate both days.

Dog shows, and the activities often offered along with them, such as junior showmanship, obedience, and agility, are held most frequently near metropolitan areas. So if you live near Chicago and Peggy wants to compete in obedience, there will be ample opportunities within an hour or so from home. But if you live farther out, you may have to drive two or three hours to attend a dog show. On the other hand, hunting tests, lure coursing, and herding require wide open spaces. So if you live in the city and Kevin wants to attend hunting tests, expect to drive well over an hour.

Whether traveling near or far, give yourself a good map and plenty of time. Then enjoy the scenery and the opportunity to spend uninterrupted time with Peggy or Kevin.

LESSONS

No matter which activities appeal to Peggy and Kevin, they will have to learn two essentials: how to train their dogs for their chosen activities and how to properly handle their dogs during tests, trials, or shows. That means they will need lessons, and possibly some equipment, and transportation to and fro.

How long your child will need lessons depends on many factors. Different activities require different amounts of training. For example, passing the first level of the lure coursing or earthdog programs demands a dog with instinct, but takes very little training at all. On the other hand, passing the first level of obedience or agility doesn't demand a dog with any particular instinct, but requires considerable training and handling skill. Another variable is how high a goal Peggy and Kevin set for themselves. No matter what the activity, learning how to train and handle at each progressive level will require additional instruction.

Membership in a 4-H club is an excellent and inexpensive way for kids to learn dog care and training and begin competing in dog events. The most frequent offerings of 4-H clubs are obedience training and junior showmanship, and it makes no difference if the dogs are purebred or not. Many 4-H clubs also include agility and Canine Good Citizen, while a few perform animal-assisted therapy and encourage projects such as raising a puppy for an organization that provides service dogs for the handicapped.

All-breed dog clubs, obedience clubs, and specialty clubs (clubs dedicated to one particular breed) are also good possibilities for finding training and handling instruction. While more costly than 4-H, dog club classes are usually quite affordable. Details on locating clubs dedicated to your child's activity are in the chapter on that activity.

Some activities will take more training, equipment, and overall time and expense than others, depending on where you live and what the activities are. Training a retriever for hunting tests will be more time-consuming for an urban dweller than for a kid in the country.

Many privately owned dog training schools offer excellent beginner classes, as well as advanced work geared toward competitive events. Sometimes they are a little more expensive than club-sponsored lessons, but they may be more convenient. Dog training schools can be found in the yellow pages of your telephone book.

PRACTICE

Perfecting any sport takes practice, and some dog activities take far more practice than others, but long practice sessions are never beneficial. You may wonder if the kids are losing interest when you see them go outside to practice and return in fifteen minutes or less, but they are probably following their instructor's advice.

Lia Ann Temarantz poses with her Toy Poodle, Rachel, and a dumbbell, part of obedience competition equipment. Courtesy of Temarantz Studio.

Fifteen minutes makes an ideal practice session for many dog events, and more would be worse, not better. Good trainers learn to read their dogs (know when they're enjoying the training and when they show the first signs of fatigue). "Don't bore your dog" and "Quit while your dog is still enjoying itself" are training rules Peggy and Kevin may frequently hear from their instructors. That's because in dog activities too much practice doesn't make perfect. Instead, it makes for a drab performance.

Since every event and every dog necessitates a different amount of training, it's best to let Kevin and Peggy set up their own flexible training schedules. If you want to assess their interest and abilities, evaluate the creativity they put into their practice sessions and the improvement you see in their actual performances—not the amount of time they spend on simple repetition.

The practice sessions of most concern are the ones children under driving age need transportation to attend. A few dog activities, such as agility and lure coursing, involve a great deal of equipment—more than most families care to own or have room to store. Others, like herding and hunting tests, involve the use of livestock or game birds and a great deal of space. Although some basics for these activities can be reviewed at home, practice sessions with the proper equipment or livestock are essential. In fact, even activities such as obedience and junior showmanship can't be perfected by practicing only in the backyard. Before competing, Rex needs the opportunity to practice in several different locations, often in the company of strangers and other dogs. This is called proofing, and it means teaching Rex to focus on his work, even in the midst of distractions.

In addition to holding classes, some dog clubs and training schools set up practice schedules and provide equipment. Expect to pay a fee for practices, in addition to providing transportation. Sometimes parents take turns carpooling kids and dogs to practices, but many parents enjoy the ride. They say the drive is quality time—an opportunity for conversation without interference from telephones or television.

Chapter 2

Why Bother? (What Will Dog Activities Do for My Children?)

Transportation! Lessons! Equipment! Yikes! Does Kevin really have to participate in structured activities with his new dog, Ginger? Why can't Peggy just take Rex for a nice walk every day after school? Isn't that good enough?

Yes, a daily walk is good enough to give Peggy exercise (and Rex, too), but like any activity that remains the same day after day, it may soon become a mindless mission. In fact, when the weather is nice, walking the dog will probably rank somewhat higher than vacuuming or unloading the dishwasher, and when the weather is nasty, it may rank somewhat lower.

Organized activities, on the other hand, are interesting and exciting, as they offer the challenge of developing new skills. So if Peggy is dog-crazy, count your blessings. Children who are deeply involved in dog activities learn responsibility, leadership, sportsmanship, confidence, and many more fine attributes that remain with them throughout their lives. So let's take a look at the bright side of giving up some time and spending some money so Peggy and Kevin can participate in organized events with Rex and Ginger. While preparing their dogs for any type of activity, what will your kids learn?

TEAMWORK

When Peggy and Rex join an organized program, one of the first things Peggy will learn is that teamwork is essential. She and Rex will be encouraged to communicate with each other and work together smoothly. A good instructor will teach Peggy how to "read" Rex (understand his feelings through watching his body language), and she will soon realize that Rex is constantly "reading" her. That's fascinating enough, but there is also the possibility of an additional bonus. As young people become aware of the messages their body language sends to their dogs, they are more apt to understand the messages careless manners or poor posture may send to people.

11

Children who are deeply involved in dog activities learn responsibility, leadership, sportsmanship, confidence, and many more fine attributes that remain with them throughout their lives.

Self-help books on climbing the corporate ladder almost always stress the importance of being a team player. Some of those books say this puts women at a disadvantage, because boys generally participate in more team sports while growing up than girls do. Training a dog gives girls and boys a chance to learn teamwork, whether or not they play on a school team. As for dog lovers who are earning varsity letters, teamwork is an attribute that is impossible to overdo.

Attending classes with a dog doesn't only teach teamwork with the dog, but also with the teacher and other students. The instructor can't be everywhere at once, so students who have perfected a lesson often help those who need a little more practice. During one session, Peggy may take on the roles of student and teacher and discover that helping others perfect the lesson, and seeing their eyes light up with understanding, can be nearly as rewarding as mastering it herself.

RESPONSIBILITY

Do you wish Kevin would take on more responsibility around the house? Organized programs, like those offered by 4-H clubs, include instruction on feeding, grooming, preventive medicine, and exercise. Most members of the club can't wait to practice their new skills on their dogs, and peer pressure acts as a positive force that helps these programs work. Motivated by his instructors and his fellow club members, Kevin may soon want full responsibility for feeding, brushing, and exercising Ginger. It may not be a typical household chore like mowing the lawn or bagging the leaves, but it's a beginning.

Learning an activity with a dog promotes teamwork and responsibility.

CONFIDENCE BUILDING

As Peggy becomes deeply involved in dog activities and makes friends in her field, she will develop a strong sense of identity and purpose. This will go a long way toward developing the strength of character all children need to help them stand up to negative peer pressure.

Success in their sport is a real confidence booster, and even a little bit of it will keep kids motivated. This is Darcie Peterson and Innisglen Peppermint Rainbow, CDX (Peppy, for short).

Success builds confidence, and good dog training programs are built on a foundation of setting short- and long-term goals and achieving them one step at a time. As Rex perfects each portion of an exercise, Peggy will enjoy the satisfaction that comes from attaining a goal. Later, when all the steps combine to create a polished whole, she will glow with a sense of accomplishment.

Every dog activity in this book will eventually take Peggy and Rex someplace where they will use their new abilities in either demonstrations, tests, or competitive events. Participating will teach Peggy to concentrate and remain poised while performing for an audience or a judge. No matter how severe her initial stage fright, she will conquer it in time, if only for Rex's sake, as dogs perform best for calm handlers.

Like chocolate, success is sweet and rather addictive, and once kids find out how to get it, they always want it. Learning how to set short- and long-term goals, break down large projects into doable parts, and handle the pressure of performing in public could help Peggy succeed in many fields.

COMMUNICATION WITH ALL AGES

Making friends across generations is easiest when everyone has the same hobby in common, and while participating in dog activities, Kevin will meet people of all ages with similar interests. In fact, there are more adults than kids at most dog events, and since many adults consider youngsters the future of dog sports, they are helpful and supportive. Even if Kevin is usually retiring, and finds it hard to talk to adults, dog events will give him no choice. He will have to interact with his instructor and the other students (often adults), and later with judges, various officials, and fellow competitors.

Best of all (in some cases), Kevin may soon have more to say at home. He'll probably want to show you what Ginger just learned, and may chat about his instructor and the other students and dogs in the class. In fact, many parents credit dog activities with enhancing the communication, and hence the relationship, between them and their children.

PRODUCTIVE USE OF TIME

Kids and dogs are both happiest when they are engrossed in doing something positive. With lessons and practice sessions in addition to homework and other activities, Peggy will soon learn how to manage

Your kids and dogs will both be happiest when they're engrossed in doing something fun. These boys have built a tunnel for their terrier to practice earthdog tests (discussed in chapter 18).

her time so nothing important is missed. Of course, she will have less free time. Kids who are busily working at a project of their choosing seldom find time just to hang out.

PATIENCE

In a world where faster is often synonymous with better, it can be difficult for kids to learn the importance of patience. But there aren't any shortcuts in the step-by-step progression of dog training. Patience and persistence, not speed, determine success. Coming to terms with this prepares children for the long-term projects they may encounter as adults—the most important of which may be parenthood.

SPORTSMANSHIP

Competitive dog events provide frequent opportunities for children to learn how to win graciously and turn losses into valuable learning experiences. However, it doesn't just happen. Since kids take their cues from the adults they most respect, it's important that parents and instructors set the example.

Referees, umpires, and dog event judges all make mistakes some-times, and kids should understand that while a poor decision is unfor-tunate, it's just part of the game, not the end of the world. When Kevin's emphasis is on setting personal goals and trying to better his own performance, he'll know how well he did before the winners are announced, and won't let an occasional poor decision ruin his day. Smiling and congratulating the winners should be obligatory, even if today's winners don't have the sense to reciprocate tomorrow when the trophy is in Kevin's hand.

LEADERSHIP

Is Peggy a follower and you wish she were a leader? Chances are she doesn't want to lead because she isn't ready yet. But don't worry. Innumerable kids who were followers in junior high became president of their college class.

While there's no point in trying to prod Peggy into leadership before she's comfortable in that role, you can guide her into activities where she'll have an opportunity to lead when she's ready. In fact, even if she wants to lead, she'll need some special knowledge or talent to be accepted as a leader. The peer group puts kids in leadership posi-tions only when other kids admire them enough to want to follow.

A good 4-H club encourages qualities such as knowledge, skill, and poise, and these attributes form the basis of leadership. In addition to training their dogs, 4-H kids give demonstrations and sometimes oral presentations. As children progress, they may be asked to help teach newer kids and may eventually become junior or teen leaders.

Many other dog activities also enhance leadership skills and give kids the confidence to visualize themselves as future leaders. Animal-assisted therapy and service dog puppy raiser programs make kids feel good about themselves while motivating them to interact with other people. In fact, succeeding at any dog sport will not only enhance Peggy's self-image, but will inspire other kids to place Peggy in a leadership role by asking her how she trained Rex to do this or that. As she gives them some training tips and they follow her advice, Peggy will have her first experience of real leadership—being placed in the position of teacher by her peers.

Chapter 3

Evaluating Your Child

as Jessie been talking about joining a 4-H dog project? Does Eric want to learn how to train the family retriever? Does Dawn beg for a dog before every birthday and holiday? Are you getting close to giving in?

Is there a way to determine if your kids will remain devoted to dog ventures long enough to make your commitment count? And how can you help your children decide which activities will be most enjoyable for them?

The following evaluation may help. Just circle the answers that most nearly fit your child, and read the interpretation that follows. Since every child is unique, with an exclusive set of preferences and attributes, there are no right or wrong answers—just different ones.

1. My child would rather

   (a) participate in an outdoor game or sport

   (b) play a video game or board game with friends indoors

   (c) watch television

2. My child prefers to be

   (a) with lots of friends

   (b) with one or two best friends

   (c) alone

3. On vacation, my child prefers sleeping

   (a) in a tent at a campsite

   (b) in a motel

19

4. For a science project, my child usually chooses something

> *(a) alive, that needs constant tending, such as seedlings*
>
> *(b) inanimate, that can be proven quickly, such as electrical current*

5. My child's favorite books are

> *(a) animal stories*
>
> *(b) adventures or mysteries*
>
> *(c) romances*

6. My child would rather

> *(a) go hiking, fishing, or camping*
>
> *(b) work with the computer or play computer games with friends*
>
> *(c) go to a movie*

7. My child

> *(a) runs the half mile to visit a friend*
>
> *(b) walks the half mile to visit a friend*
>
> *(c) asks me to drive him/her to visit a friend*

8. My child is

> *(a) outgoing*
>
> *(b) reserved*
>
> *(c) shy*

9. My child regularly plays

> *(a) team sports, such as baseball, football, basketball, or volleyball*
>
> *(b) individual sports, such as running, tennis, in-line skating, skateboarding, or horseback riding*
>
> *(c) no sports on a regular basis*

10. When it rains, my child

   (a) continues his/her outdoor activities as if nothing has changed

   (b) changes into suitable clothes and continues his/her outside activity

   (c) comes inside immediately and stays in

   (d) doesn't notice, because he/she is seldom outside in the first place

11. My child easily holds conversations with

   (a) people of all ages

   (b) his/her peers

   (c) no one at the moment

12. My child takes lessons, such as piano, guitar, or dancing,

   (a) twice a week or more

   (b) once a week

   (c) never

Answer #13 only if your answer to #12 was (a) or (b).

13. My child practices

   (a) without being told

   (b) when reminded

   (c) when nagged or screamed at

   (d) when threatened with losing privileges

14. My child does his/her homework

   (a) faithfully

   (b) when reminded

   (c) when nagged or screamed at

   (d) when threatened with losing privileges

15. My child participates in _____ extracurricular activity(ies), such as band, team sports, student government, or cheerleading.

   (a) two or more

   (b) one

   (c) no

16. My child thinks school is

   (a) great

   (b) okay

   (c) boring

   (d) awful

17. My child usually

   (a) finishes school projects ahead of schedule

   (b) finishes school projects on time

   (c) finishes school projects at 3:00 a.m. on the morning they are due

   (d) turns in school projects late

   (e) fails to complete school projects

18. My child's grades are mostly

   (a) As and Bs

   (b) Bs and Cs

   (c) Cs and Ds

19. My child has enjoyed the same hobby for

   (a) three years or more

   (b) one to three years

   (c) less than a year

   (d) doesn't have a hobby

20. My child performs his/her household chores

>   *(a) automatically, without being told*
>
>   *(b) right away, upon being reminded*
>
>   *(c) only after I nag or scream*
>
>   *(d) only under threat of no television or being grounded*

21. My child has changed hobbies _____ times in the past two years.

>   *(a) zero (He/she kept the same hobby.)*
>
>   *(b) one to two*
>
>   *(c) two to three*
>
>   *(d) four or more*
>
>   *(e) zero (He/she had no hobbies in the last two years.)*

22. When my child interacts with a dog, he/she

>   *(a) talks to the dog and pets it for five minutes or more*
>
>   *(b) talks to and/or pets the dog for a minute or two*
>
>   *(c) gives the dog a quick pat then ignores it*

23. When my child plays with a dog, he/she

>   *(a) tries to teach the dog a trick*
>
>   *(b) tries to get it to play ball games, such as keep-away, catch, or fetch*
>
>   *(c) enjoys running, chasing, wrestling, or tug games with it*
>
>   *(d) loses interest quickly*

24. My child's room has _____ pictures of dogs decorating the walls.

>   *(a) more than three*
>
>   *(b) two or three*
>
>   *(c) one or two*
>
>   *(d) no*

If there is no dog in your family, please skip the next eight questions and begin again at question 33.

If there is a dog in your family, please continue. Your final question is #32.

25. When my child comes home from school, he/she

    (a) fusses over the dog immediately

    (b) greets the dog briefly

    (c) pushes the dog away if it demands too much attention

26. When my child's friends are visiting, he/she

    (a) includes the dog in the group

    (b) includes the dog until it becomes a pest

    (c) shuts the dog out of the room

27. My child _____ remembers and celebrates the dog's birthday.

    (a) always

    (b) sometimes

    (c) never

28. My child

    (a) always remembers to walk the dog

    (b) walks the dog whenever asked

    (c) tries to get out of walking the dog

29. My child has taught the dog

    (a) several tricks

    (b) a trick or two

    (c) nothing

30. My child has

    (a) occasionally put clothes on the dog just for fun

    (b) dressed the dog up for Halloween

    (c) never tried to dress the dog

31. My child brushes the dog

    (a) often

    (b) when reminded or asked

    (c) never

32. When my child comes home from school, the dog

    (a) gets incredibly excited and stays right with him/her

    (b) greets him/her happily but briefly

    (c) wags its tail a little but doesn't bother to get up

    (d) looks the other way or goes into a different room

33. We have no dog, but my child has begged for one

    (a) for as long as I can remember

    (b) occasionally, when nothing else takes precedence

    (c) recently

    (d) never, but I wish he/she were interested in dog activities

34. My child talks about dogs

    (a) incessantly

    (b) occasionally

    (c) seldom

35. Ever since he/she was little, my child drew many pictures of

    (a) animals

    (b) people

    (c) cars, airplanes, or boats

36. On the subject of dogs, my child

> *(a) constantly surprises me with his/her knowledge of breed identification, care, training, and other facts*
>
> *(b) occasionally teaches me something I never knew*
>
> *(c) seldom says anything*

37. My child has a pet other than a dog and

> *(a) takes total responsibility for its food and care*
>
> *(b) takes care of it when reminded*
>
> *(c) often forgets and I take care of the pet*

38. Concerning his/her friends' dogs, my child remembers

> *(a) their names, breeds, ages, and habits*
>
> *(b) their names*
>
> *(c) very little*

iNTERPRETiNG YOUR ANSWERS

PREFERENCES AND ATTITUDES

Questions #1 through #11 evaluate your child's preferences and attitudes.

Characteristics that many dog sports have in common are that they make physical and mental demands on the trainer, are rather social, involve tests or competition, and are held outdoors no matter what the weather. A large number of (a) answers signifies an outdoorsy, active, and highly social child who would probably excel at almost any canine endeavor, provided he or she has the desire, and the dog is suitable for the activity. Special favorites might be agility, junior showmanship, animal-assisted therapy, tracking, or one of the sporting events that showcase his or her dog's inherited talents. This child may be somewhat overconfident and consequently not practice quite enough, but the sport of dogs will soon teach the child that even naturals need preparation to win.

Mostly (b) answers, with some (a) answers mixed in, indicate a child who is a bit more reserved and possibly a little less confident. If this child has a lot of desire, he or she will work very hard without being prodded and be highly successful if teamed with a suitable dog. In addition, the child will benefit from meeting a wide variety of people and will probably increase his or her activity level and love of the outdoors. Favorite activities might be obedience or dog showing, as well as sporting events testing the dog's natural talents. Becoming a puppy raiser for a service dog organization or participating in animal-assisted therapy would boost this child's self-esteem and social skills.

Several (c) answers with some (b) answers mixed in denote a child who may be quite shy, has a low activity level, or doesn't like outdoor activities. While this child may not enjoy extremely physical endeavors, such as agility, or trips through the woods or fields for performance tests, the sport of obedience might be just the ticket. When motivated by a strong desire to work with a dog, this child may absolutely blossom. As he or she accomplishes each progressive goal, the child will become more secure and consequently more active and outgoing. In fact, obedience could be just the beginning. If this child advances to endeavors such as animal-assisted therapy, the child will receive as many benefits as he or she gives.

RESPONSIBILITY AND ATTENTION SPAN

Questions #12 through #21 evaluate your child's sense of responsibility and attention span.

Mostly (a) and (b) answers indicate a child who is busy, has varied interests, takes responsibility for his or her actions, finishes what he or she starts, enjoys learning, and makes good use of time. This child has already developed the habits that lead to success, and needs only an occasional reminder to complete responsibilities. If your child fits this description and has a strong desire to participate in dog events, chances are excellent that your child will take good care of the pet and succeed at the dog sport of his or her choice.

A few (c) answers, in addition to some (a) and/or (b) answers, signify a child who may still be searching for an activity exciting enough to stimulate continuing interest. If this child scores high in the next category, degree of desire, then participating in dog events could enhance his or her sense of responsibility and attention span, causing improvement in many areas, including school. In fact, membership in the right 4-H group could have a marvelous effect on this child's attitude toward responsibility. But beware. If this child's desire isn't very strong, he or she may tire of dog events quickly and you will end up taking care of the dog or nagging your child to do so.

Several (c) answers, along with a couple of (d) or (e) answers, denote a child who has not yet developed a sense of responsibility or found a lasting field of interest, and is falling behind in school due to inattention or boredom. If your child fits this description, but scores high on desire and is absolutely hounding you for the opportunity to work with a dog, give the request some serious consideration. Attending dog-training classes won't make this child fall further behind with school work, and may be exactly what it takes to awaken his or her interest and sense of responsibility. But if this child scores low in desire, don't get a dog just because you think it will help. It probably won't, and the dog will simply become an additional chore. Instead, try to help your child discover his or her real field of interest. Once your child becomes deeply involved in a productive hobby of his or her own choosing, your child's attention span and sense of responsibility should gradually improve.

INTEREST AND DESIRE

Questions #22 through #38 evaluate your child's degree of interest in dogs and desire to participate in dog activities. **Questions #22 through #32** evaluate children who already have a dog, while **questions #22 through #24 and #33 through #38** evaluate children who do not have a dog.

A combination of (a) and (b) answers reveal children who definitely have dogs on their mind. If your child already owns a dog, he or she probably trained the dog to do a few tricks and often includes it in games and social activities. The child who does not have a dog reads dog books, knows about care and the importance of training, and talks fondly about friends' pets. Either child is highly motivated and a good candidate to enjoy responsible dog ownership and participate in canine activities.

A combination of mostly (b) and (c) answers indicates children who enjoy dogs when they are in the mood for them but may soon get over the novelty of daily dog care or regular practice. If your child fits this description but has a well-developed sense of responsibility and wants to participate in a canine activity, give it a try if you already have a dog. The structured training, along with the excitement of accomplishment and the promise of competition, may soon make your child and dog into an inseparable team. But if you don't have a dog, getting one is not a step that can be taken lightly. A puppy is not a disposable object like a used guitar or the piano nobody plays. A dog deserves love, care, and a permanent home, and giving it anything less sends your child a sorry message. So, unless you are getting a dog because you want one in the family, don't acquire one solely for a child whose evaluation placed him or her in this category. Instead, pay close attention to your child's conversations over the next six months to a year, and then evaluate him or her again.

Mostly (c) answers with an occasional (d) suggest a child who has little interest in dogs or dog activities. Don't acquire a dog for this child unless you want one for yourself. If you already have a dog and your child asks to take it to training classes, read on.

"In 1990 my mom borrowed a dog for me to train for the summer, as she wasn't sure of my dedication to training," says Dustin Peterson, age 14, of Opheim, Illinois. "Clyde, the Coonhound, was a training challenge, but I learned a lot from him. We ended up taking first place in our class at the county fair. We even traveled to Springfield, Illinois, for the state fair. Clyde couldn't take the stress and noise and broke his down-stay, but we had a good time.

Dustin's dedication, patience, and practice paid off. In 1994, he and his Sheltie, Nikki, won Grand Champion Obedience Dog at the county 4-H fair and also Grand Champion Junior Handler in showmanship. They also earned a Companion Dog title at AKC shows.

"A little more assured of my dedication, Mom rescued a Sheltie in 1991 and presented her to me. She was one huge mat of hair, covered with fleas, tips of her ears bare from fly bites, and nearly ready to whelp a litter of puppies. It took a lot of patience and time, but Nikki finally settled down to obedience training. She is a soft dog and harsh corrections are a no-no, a bit different from Clyde!"

PASSING THE TEST

Still confused about whether or not Dawn should have a dog? Still wondering if Eric will finally stick with a hobby? If Eric or Dawn scored low on responsibility or desire, or have changed hobbies so often that you don't want to pay for any more lessons, there is a program that will test their staying power as dog trainers without requiring outside instruction. It's called the Canine Good Citizen program (see chapter 7) and it consists of a 10-part test to determine if a dog has enough basic training to be an upstanding member of the community.

Although it's easier to train for this test by attending classes, a determined youngster at least 10 years old (with a suitable dog) should be able to follow the free instructions, train his or her dog, and pass the test. Since Eric already has a dog, he could use the test to prove his perseverance. Dawn can get the instructions, explain the program to a relative or friend with an untrained dog, and ask if she may train his or her pet and handle the dog at a test. If Dawn and Eric manage this feat on their own, they have demonstrated their desire and ability to succeed in dog events, and deserve to own dogs and attend classes in their chosen activities.

Chapter 4

Evaluating Your Dog

G us loves to do tricks for the family, but how will he do in the obedience ring when large crowds are watching? Ginger is a fine lap warmer, but is she capable of warming hearts as a therapy dog? Odie jumps high enough to scare squirrels away from the bird feeder, but does he have the temperament to be competitive in agility?

No matter how much potential your child has, the four-legged member of the team must be suitable, or both partners will become frustrated. This evaluation will help you decide if the family pet is a likely candidate for dog activities and, if so, which events may be its forte. Just circle the answers that most nearly fit the family dog, and read the interpretation that follows.

For whatever activity your child chooses, if the four-footed member of the team isn't suitable (for any number of reasons), both partners will become frustrated. This little girl and her Lhasa Apso have earned obedience ribbons by being a real team.

1. Our dog lives

   (a) indoors

   (b) indoors, but spends a lot of time in the yard

   (c) outdoors

2. Our dog prefers the company of

   (a) children and adults equally

   (b) children best, but adults are okay

   (c) adults only

3. Our dog likes

   (a) men and women equally

   (b) most women, but shies away from some men

   (c) only people he/she knows well

4. When invited to ride in the car, our dog

   (a) is excited and happy

   (b) is neutral and calm

   (c) is unhappy, scared, or carsick

5. Our dog's tail

   (a) seems to never stop wagging

   (b) is generally relaxed

   (c) is often between his/her legs

6. When company arrives, our dog

   (a) likes attention but minds his manners

   (b) is an overly friendly nuisance

   (c) is quiet and subdued, possibly even a bit frightened

7. When passing a strange dog on the street, our dog

   (a) either ignores it or wants to play

   (b) acts aggressive and barks or growls with hackles up

   (c) becomes shy and tries to hide behind me

8. When someone rings the bell, our dog

    (a) walks to the door with me and stays beside me

    (b) races happily to the door, hoping the visitor will play with him/her

    (c) usually ignores it

    (d) runs to the door in a barking, growling rage

9. At feeding time, our dog

    (a) eats up all his/her dog food quickly

    (b) eats a little bit at a time and takes more than 15 minutes to finish his/her dinner

    (c) hardly eats at all

10. Our dog

    (a) is relaxed in a dog crate

    (b) is nervous about being in a dog crate

    (c) has never been in a dog crate

11. When I have to leave our dog in the boarding kennel or the veterinary clinic, he/she

    (a) does just fine

    (b) is upset at first, but eventually adjusts

    (c) loses weight from pacing, crying, and refusing food

12. Our dog is afraid of

    (a) nothing

    (b) thunder

    (c) strangers

    (d) sudden loud noises

    (e) crowds

    (f) larger dogs

13. When something startles our dog, he/she

    (a) recovers immediately

    (b) is a bit nervous for five minutes or less

    (c) takes more than five minutes to get back to normal

14. Our dog

    (a) *loves to be groomed and is even calm when his/her toenails are clipped*

    (b) *allows him/herself to be groomed, but is glad when it's over*

    (c) *hates being groomed and sometimes tries to resist*

15. When it rains, our dog

    (a) *steps into every puddle*

    (b) *doesn't seem to mind*

    (c) *refuses to go out*

16. Our dog would most enjoy

    (a) *a long run in a field or the woods*

    (b) *a walk around the block*

    (c) *a long nap on a soft rug*

17. Our dog plays with his/her toys

    (a) *often*

    (b) *occasionally*

    (c) *almost never*

18. Our dog's age is

    (a) *between two months and two years*

    (b) *between two years and five years*

    (c) *over five years*

19. Our dog

    (a) *was easy to housebreak*

    (b) *was hard to housebreak*

    (c) *still isn't completely housebroken*

20. Our dog

    (a) *knows four or more tricks*

    (b) *knows between one and three tricks*

    (c) *was never taught any tricks*

21. If I give a simple command, such as "Sit," in a normal tone of voice, our dog

    (a) sits

    (b) makes me repeat it a few times in a louder voice before he/she sits

    (c) doesn't know what I mean because he/she has never been trained to sit

22. Our dog's health is

    (a) excellent

    (b) average

    (c) helping the veterinarian make payments on his Mercedes

23. When our dog is allowed off leash in a safe new place, he/she

    (a) explores, but doesn't stray far

    (b) stays by our side

    (c) runs off and goes exploring, leaving us behind

24. Our dog

    (a) gets excited at the sight of a squirrel or rabbit, but is still controllable

    (b) indicates the animal's presence, but would rather be in my lap than chase it

    (c) goes absolutely wild at the sight of a squirrel or rabbit

    (d) seldom gets excited about anything

25. Our dog could best be described as

    (a) playful

    (b) affectionate

    (c) hyper

    (d) sleepy

26. If I toss a ball, our dog usually

    (a) chases it and brings it back to me

    (b) chases it and plays with it a little

    (c) ignores it

27. In the house, our dog

   (a) is constantly underfoot

   (b) usually follows a family member from room to room

   (c) spends a lot of time sleeping

28. One of our dog's habits is

   (a) carrying things around in his/her mouth

   (b) chasing leaves, bits of paper, or anything else that blows by

   (c) circling, barking, or nipping at heels in an effort to keep children or other pets together in a group

   (d) digging holes

29. Our dog's movements are

   (a) graceful, agile, and quick

   (b) solid and steady, but rather slow

   (c) so awkward and clumsy they make us laugh

   (d) stiff and hesitant

30. Our dog

   (a) is especially careful around babies and frail people

   (b) treats everyone the same

   (c) sometimes roughhouses too hard for the person playing with him/her

31. On walks, our dog's nose

   (a) doesn't do anything in particular

   (b) is usually held high, sniffing the air

   (c) is usually low, sniffing the ground

32. In a crowd of people, our dog

   (a) shows off or wants to play

   (b) acts the same way he/she always does

   (c) becomes nervous or afraid

33. If there is a low obstacle, such as a log, in our dog's path, he/she will

   (a) jump it

   (b) scamper over it

   (c) walk around it

34. In the yard, our dog

   (a) often races around at top speed for no reason

   (b) loves to chase squirrels and rabbits

   (c) soon whines at the door to come back in the house

35. Our dog is

   (a) a purebred with registration papers

   (b) a purebred without registration papers

   (c) a mixed breed

iNTERPRETiNG YoUR ANSWERS

TEMPERAMENT (DISPOSITION)

Temperament is evaluated in **questions #1 through #15.**

Your pet's temperament is shaped by his heredity and environment. While you can't change your pet's heredity, you have already influenced his temperament and will continue to do so.

Question #1, for example, asks where your dog lives. If you answered (a), chances are excellent that your dog relates to people much better than if you answered (c). Dog (b) might also be quite social. It depends on whether or not his indoor time is spent with the family.

Dog activities may be held at the county fairgrounds, the Houston Astrodome, or the field just outside of town, but they all have a few things in common. The dog has to get there in a vehicle, remain manageable around strange dogs and crowds of people, perform for an audience, and, depending on the event, be touched by strangers. Dogs that were socialized as puppies (introduced to many people and places, and taken along on family excursions) quickly learn to take events in stride, while unsocialized dogs may be fearful, defensive, or aggressive.

Questions #1 to #15. If your dog rates mostly (a) and only a few (b) answers, he has the temperament to handle dog activities and will probably adore the added attention. Dogs with nearly all (b) answers will also do fine, provided your child is patient and trains thoroughly, especially around distractions. These dogs may be somewhat stressed at their first few outings, but will soon learn to love the exciting bustle of dog events.

If your dog rated several (c) or (d) answers, and is fearful of nearly everything in question 12, he is not a good candidate for dog activities. That doesn't mean your dog can't succeed if given patient training and lots of socialization, because he can. Many children have rescued unwanted dogs with temperament quirks and made winners of them, but it isn't easy. If your child accepts such a challenge, try to understand that simply doing the activity with the pet may be more of an accomplishment than winning first place with a more suitable dog.

ACTIVITY LEVEL

Questions #16, #17, and #18 evaluate your dog's activity level.

Some dog events demand an enthusiastic animal in prime physical condition. For other activities, a healthy if somewhat passive pet will do just fine. Dogs in the (a) and (b) categories should do well in obedience, agility, therapy, junior showmanship, dog showing, and tracking. Sleepy (c) dogs make exceptional pet-therapy prospects once they are obedience trained, and may enjoy tracking and junior showmanship. If your dog received a (c) only on question 18, ignore it for now. Dogs, like people, are only as old as they act. Situations where the dog slows down due to age, while the child is still deeply involved in dog sports, are covered later in this chapter.

All of the sporting events designed to test a dog's natural instincts, such as hunting, herding, lure coursing, and earthdog events, are best performed by eager, excited dogs, the kind that received two or more (a) answers. Does that leave your (c) dog yawning on the rug? Not necessarily. Activities that rely on a dog's instincts sometimes wake up sleeping passions. Many young owners who tried sporting events with their lazy dogs were elated when their pets had a change of attitude and were raring to go. There's no harm in letting your child try if he or she wants to, provided the dog is in good physical condition.

TRAINABILITY

Questions #19, #20, and #21 evaluate your dog's trainability.

A dog that has been trained to do something, even if the training took place a long time ago, has learned how to learn. Such a dog is generally easier to train than a dog that has never been taught any-thing. Dogs rating all (a) answers will be easiest to train for a new activity, while (b) dogs may need a little more work to achieve the same degree of success. A (c) dog may prove quite difficult for a young trainer, unless the dog is still a puppy. Young puppies make ideal train-ing candidates.

TEMPERAMENT, ACTIVITY LEVEL, AND TRAINABILITY

A combination of characteristics, composed of temperament, activity level, and trainability, are evaluated in **questions #22 through #25**.

Mostly (a) and (b) answers denote a dog that is suitable for a wide variety of activities. Mostly (c) and (d) answers indicate a dog that may be difficult to train.

POTENTIAL FOR SPECIAL ACTIVITIES

Questions #26 through #35 may help you discover your dog's special talents. Of course, temperament, activity level, and trainability still play an important role in determining your dog's potential for success.

All (a) answers from questions 26 through 28 indicate a dog with a strong potential to succeed in the sport of obedience. A (b) answer to question 28, along with (a) answers on questions 29 and 34, de-note lure coursing possibilities. Herding potential may show up in a (c) on question 28 and an (a) on 29. If you answered (a) on questions 29, 32, 33, and 34, your dog may excel in agility.

The hole digger that received a (d) on question 28, a (c) on 31, and a (b) on 34, may become a fine earthdog. Dogs that enjoy show-ing off make the best prospects for junior showmanship and dog show-ing, so look for an (a) on question 32, although a (b) is also suitable. An ideal therapy dog will get an (a) on question 30 and a (b) on 32, but if those scores reverse, he still has plenty of therapy potential.

An (a) on questions 26 and 28, either a (b) or a (c) on 31, and an (a) or a (b) on 33, could be signs of a dog with hunting test potential. A (c) on question 31 indicates strong tracking potential.

It's great to have a dog with natural talent, but it's important to remember that several activities were designed so dogs of all shapes, sizes, and instincts could master them. Using good training techniques, all healthy dogs with stable temperaments can learn obedience, agility, junior showmanship, and tracking. They can also pass their Canine Good Citizen test and perform pet-assisted therapy.

On the other hand, no matter how well your dog scored on potential for lure coursing, he must be a registered sighthound to be eligible for this event. In fact, each of the activities testing natural instinct (hunting, lure coursing, earthdog, and herding) are open only to registered dogs that were bred for that instinct. Mixed breed dogs displaying special talents may be able to participate in activities through the American Mixed Breed Obedience Registry (see appendix I).

MISMATCHES

You've evaluated your child and the family dog and now you know. You know you have a responsible, active, outdoorsy child who can't wait to try agility, and a sleepy, sweet, older dog with a weak knee from a long-forgotten injury. Or maybe you have a "who's handling who?" situation—a young, slightly shy youngster and a huge, high-spirited dog.

Mismatches need serious thought, because trying to train an unsuitable dog will frustrate your child and be unfair to the dog, and could have a negative effect on the child-dog relationship. Discuss the dog's problems (too old, too big and strong, not the right breed for the chosen activity) with your child, being sure to speak of the dog as a beloved family member, not like a cracked baseball bat that should be discarded and replaced. Talk about solutions together. Naturally, the possibility of acquiring a second dog will be brought up, and, depending on your location and lifestyle, it may be the perfect solution. If your child is truly responsible, and serious about dog sports, your child's most valuable asset for success is a puppy of his or her own. Get one young enough (between seven and eight weeks is ideal) so your child can socialize him thoroughly, and encourage your child to choose a breed, or type of dog, that will make a suitable partner for the child's favorite dog sports.

Not everyone can get a second dog, so compromises are essential. Sleepy, sweet, older dogs can still learn enough basic obedience to become involved in animal-assisted therapy. In fact, they sometimes become stars. A mature dog with a graying muzzle is often the popular favorite at the local nursing home, and its quiet demeanor also makes it ideal in children's hospitals. Tracking titles may also be within an older dog's reach and are certainly outdoorsy, though not quite as active as agility.

Unfortunately, the "who's handling who?" scenario has no compromise. A young, retiring child is simply not strong or assertive enough to train a huge, high-spirited dog, and such a dog needs training—the sooner the better. It looks like it may be your job. After the dog learns to obey basic commands, keep reviewing them. If your child is still interested in dog training when he or she gets a little older, the chance of succeeding in a chosen activity is better if the dog remembers a few basic commands.

Sometimes a child and a dog start out perfectly compatible, but the child advances faster than the dog. For example, an 11-year-old child and an active 6-year-old dog may perform beginning agility just beautifully together. But in a few years, the child may develop championship form and the aging dog may slow down.

Mismatches can occur in practically every dog activity. There's the junior showmanship winner who wants to exhibit in the breed ring, but doesn't have a show-quality dog. And there's the child who scored high in novice obedience and wants to train for Open, but the pet is developing cataracts and misjudges the jumps.

When a bright, young trainer enters dog sports with a middle-aged pet, the trainer may outgrow the dog sooner or later if he or she sticks with the sport. Each family has to find its own solutions. The important thing is to avoid snap decisions by being aware of the possibility in advance. Discuss the situation with your child, showing respect for both the elderly dog and your child's ambitions.

Chapter 5

Supportive Parenting

Myriad benefits await young people who become immersed in the world of dog events. And while almost every youngster gains in one way or another, those lucky enough to have supportive parents learn positive lessons that will help them succeed all their lives. Being supportive means that the parent is willing to facilitate the child's participation by driving the child to activities, purchasing supplies, and providing any necessary training and lessons.

"But it doesn't end there," according to Dr. Mary Burch, a psychologist who provides behavioral consultation to parents and school administrators and serves as Field Director of AKC's Canine Good Citizen program. "Another critical part of being supportive is for parents to provide children with positive reinforcement. This means parents should tell their children that they are proud of them and have noticed improvement in a particular area or skill. When you pinpoint a particular area where your child has shown increased proficiency, the child realizes that you are really aware of his progress, not just mouthing empty praise.

"It is important for the child's mental well-being that parents teach their children to win graciously. Nobody likes a winner who gloats, and competition of a vicious nature will result in a child who does not enjoy the sport.

"Children should also learn to lose graciously. Parents can teach a child how to view each loss as a learning experience and as a guide toward setting goals for improvement. Asking questions such as 'What do you think you should work on for next time?' can stimulate a productive and constructive discussion between you and your child.

"Probably the most important thing parents should stress to their children is that we do these activities because we love dogs and enjoy working with them. Competitors should leave the ring or the field with a smile on their face no matter what, or it's time to find another hobby."

"A dog is a responsibility," explains Stefani Frater, the teenager who wanted to help set up her club's Doggie Olympics. Her advice to other young trainers is, "If you want your dog to do well, as I do, then work with the dog yourself, without your parents teaching the dog. The dog should bond with you in training. You'll get more out of your wins because you know you taught the dog yourself.

Stefani Frater and Becca with their awards from the Hardin County Fair.

"Also, don't get worked up on just winning because you'll end up breaking your own heart. I've had more bad days than good days at shows, but every day was fun and worth it. From my bad days I've learned that it's okay to lose, and you should always be patient with your dog. If you aren't, you'll upset your dog and it won't be fun anymore. Keep a positive attitude even when you don't win and just think of what you should work on to win next time."

Diana Frater, Stefani's mom, comments, "The rewards a child can earn by developing a oneness with their dog are so special. Not only do they respond to each other, but they adapt a way of anticipating the actions of the other. Obedience, showmanship, and agility can all be an adventure. The important part for the parent is to allow the child hands-on experience of their own with no interference. If allowed to make their own mark, the results are fantastic."

LETTING CHILDREN LEARN

Stefani Frater, 14, is a member of the Hardin County Tailwaggers, a 4-H club in Ohio. In 1994, they held a Doggie Olympics at the county fair, introducing the audience to the sport of agility. Stefani and her Border Collie, Becca, won first place and were featured on two local

TV stations. In addition, Becca was named Grand Champion, and Stefani won first place for grooming and handling and first place for obedience. They had a marvelous day except for one thing.

"When my club held the Doggie Olympics," Stefani said, "I really didn't have to do anything but practice on the equipment at the weekly sessions and show up at the competition. That's one of the major downsides—sometimes adults and advisers take over much of the activity and don't give kids a chance. I simply participated and didn't help with other things because the adults organized the event for us."

Children can learn responsibility, organization, communication skills, and leadership through dog activities, but only if adults let them. When a parent or teacher takes control of an activity, it no longer belongs to the youngster. In fact, the child may become no more than an onlooker or, worse yet, an unwilling participant.

While attending Canine Good Citizen (CGC) tests held in conjunction with dog shows, Dr. Burch sees a lot of parent-child interaction. At one event she witnessed two extremes of parenting:

According to Dr. Burch, "One parent approached the CGC registration table saying to her preteen daughter, 'You need to do this with your dog right now, get up there.' Then she spoke to us for the daughter, rather than letting the girl practice skills in dealing with people.

"The girl had a lovely dog and I believe it would have passed the test had the handler not been a nervous wreck. During the test, I asked her why she was so nervous. She said she was worried about Junior Showmanship competition and wanted to get it over with first, but her mother made her take the CGC test.

"In this case, the child was probably using good judgment about when she should take the CGC. The mother's insistence that she 'get it over with now' in no way taught the child to make good choices or to plan her own schedule. The mother didn't listen when her daughter told her what would make her more comfortable as a handler.

"The girl's nerves seemed to travel down the leash and the dog became fidgety. It failed the CGC because it wouldn't sit or lay down on command. As the girl left the ring, her mother berated her. Then the mother loudly announced that the test was unfair and the dog failed because the spectators were making noise. This parent modeled horrible behavior, actually teaching her daughter to make excuses instead of improvements when she lost.

"By then I could stand it no longer and asked the mother if I could talk to her. I told her that we'd like to test the dog again the following day, and I believed the girl would be less nervous if she and the dog came to the ring alone. My suspicions were correct. The next day the dog passed the test with a calm handler."

MODEL MOM

"At the same event," Dr. Burch said, "there was a parent who did it all beautifully. She arrived at the CGC area with her daughter and they watched the test while the mother explained it to the child. Finally the mother said, 'Why don't you think about if you'd like to try it?' Then, realizing that her daughter was nervous about it, the mother suggested, 'Tell you what, I'll try it with my dog and you can watch me before you decide.'

"The mother went through the test and her dog failed. She came out of the ring smiling and said to her daughter, 'I knew I needed to work with my dog on staying in place. I'll practice and we'll pass next time.'

"Seeing her mother 'fail' so graciously apparently taught the child that you can try and fail and nothing horrible happens. So the daughter decided to try the test with her dog, and they passed.

"When the girl came out of the test area, her mother hugged her and congratulated her. Then the mother asked, 'Would you help me train my dog to stay so he can pass, too?' The child's grin got even wider as she nodded her delight.

"This is a parent who, through dog activities, teaches her child to try new things, make choices, learn through failures, and accept both winning and losing graciously. She also bolstered the child's self-esteem by asking for her help. I would guess that this child will be involved in dogs for a long time because her mother makes dog events very positive experiences. But more important than dog events," Dr. Burch concluded, "are the lessons this young girl learned about life and how to get along in this world."

HANDS OFF, BUT HEART HANDY

Backing off and letting your child set his or her own goals, plan his or her own lesson and practice schedules, take over most of the dog care and training, and decide when and where to compete isn't always easy. Chances are your child won't do these things the same way you would, and might even make some mistakes. But decision making, organizing, and goal setting all give youngsters excellent experience.

While keeping your hands off, let your child know you are on the same team by asking questions and listening to the answers. If you have never been involved in dog events, your child will enjoy explaining what Ginger has to learn in preparation for competition or tests. Ask questions that can lead to discussions, such as "Which exercise is the hardest one for Ginger so far?" and soon you may have something many parents would envy: a real conversation with your child.

This is the advice of Sharon Anderson, a training instructor with 21 years of experience in obedience and agility. Sharon is also the AKC's consultant for agility events. She lives in White Bear Lake, Minnesota. "Praise children when they do

Obedience and agility instructor Sharon Anderson (third from left), with teenage students Kate Anders, Cassie Jackson, and Jamie Watters.

well, but impress on them an appreciation for how nicely others performed, too. Most important, be sure they still love their dog as their companion win or lose. Help them understand that their dog needs constant trust and affection from them, to perform well for them. If they become good dog trainers—patient, consistent, and always train without anger and with a lot of positive motivation—they will be better prepared for the business world and for parenting themselves."

If you compete in dog events, resist the temptation to teach your child yourself, as it instantly changes the hobby from hers to yours. Even if you have more expertise than most instructors, try to find one whose methods are similar enough to yours that you can live with them, and never denigrate the instructor to your child. Class situations are best, as they promote both cooperation and the spirit of competition. Besides, they give your child a whole class full of dogs and people to tell you about. Not foisting your own methods on your child may be difficult, but being supportive without being critical could eventually pay off in a youngster who asks for your advice and wants to practice with you.

Jamie Watters praises her Border Collie, Annie.

"When I first saw Annie," says Jamie Watters, "there was an instant bond that will carry on for my entire life. She is my best friend and I love her more than anything, even boys and the telephone, and I'm a teenager." Jamie is 14 and lives in Hudson, Wisconsin.

"I guess the reason why I love working with Annie so much is because it's one-on-one. It's just me and her. If something happens and we don't do well, I always know why. It's not like school sports where it's the whole team who gets credited for winning or losing. With this sport I know that I won or I made a mistake. It's such a great feeling knowing that the reason I won is all because of my hard work.

"I really feel that the dog sport has brought my mom and I closer together. Being a teenager, it's usually hard to talk to your parents, but my mom and I have so much in common because of our dogs that we tell each other everything. My friends sometimes get upset because I'm with Annie a lot, but they love her, too, and usually understand."

COMMUNICATE

It's particularly important to know your child's goals. In the sport of obedience, for example, some handlers try to qualify and others try to win. Either one is a challenge, and the handler usually considers many factors, such as the dog's age, temperament, and breed, before setting one or the other as a goal. A parent who doesn't know which goal his child is striving for could easily make an unfortunate mistake—like offering sympathy instead of congratulations when the child earns his or her coveted qualifying score but doesn't win the class.

Of course you won't be able to say the right thing all the time, because when your child has a bad day in competition, nothing you say will be right anyway. Not to worry. Sometimes a heartfelt hug, and the reassurance that you are bursting with pride because your kid had the courage to compete, is quite enough.

Part II

Chapter 6

4-H

The name 4-H stands for head, heart, hands, and health, as described in the 4-H pledge: "I pledge my head to clearer thinking, my heart to greater loyalty, my hands to larger service, and my health to better living . . . for my club, my community, my country and my world."

4-H programs started nearly 100 years ago, with the objective of strengthening rural education for young people. Today, more than 5.4 million kids, ages 5 to 19, participate annually, and 30 percent of the membership is from metropolitan areas.

Through taking part in 4-H's affordable programs, kids acquire knowledge in a variety of areas and develop skills that are useful throughout their lives. 4-H also has a positive influence on their attitudes. By giving them an opportunity to work and compete with like-minded young people, it places kids in a situation where the peer pressure is on learning, succeeding, taking responsibility, and sharing.

Anne McNiff, 13, of Campbell, California, is wearing her 4-H uniform and practicing the long sit with her dog, Ryan. Besides training and showing two Miniature Schnauzers, Anne is a junior leader in the dog care and training project.

The backbone of 4-H is its volunteer leaders, and close to 700,000 of them deliver a variety of programs to eager kids across the nation. Of these, approximately 131,000 are junior or teen leaders. Volunteers work in partnership with County

Extension Agents, to provide educational support, leadership, and guidance. Land-grant universities house each state's 4-H headquarters, and every state has a state 4-H leader and a youth development staff, administered by the State Director of Cooperative Extension.

4-H members usually meet with their regular (general interest) club once a month. In addition, each individual project leader meets with his or her children on whatever basis they establish: weekly, bimonthly, or monthly.

DOG PROJECTS

Dog projects are one of a large selection of activities available through membership in a 4-H club. These projects vary from state to state and county to county, as they depend on the state's criteria and on the volunteer leader's areas of expertise. You can almost always count on the project including daily care, health care, and basic training. In addition, some dog projects offer one or several of the following activities: obedience, junior showmanship, agility, Canine Good Citizen, service dog puppy raiser programs, and training for animal-assisted therapy volunteers. Purebred and mixed breed dogs are both welcome in 4-H activities, and have an equal opportunity to win at competitive events. While training for these activities is also available through dog clubs or private instructors, 4-H is one of the few places where the classes are composed of young people. Most other dog training classes are predominantly made up of adults.

Youngsters are permitted to belong to a 4-H club out of their local area and may also belong to more than one, so check out the activities offered at nearby clubs to make sure your child's interests and the club's projects are a good match. To locate nearby 4-H clubs, call your state Extension Service, or simply 4-H. One or the other is probably listed under "County Government Offices" in your phone book.

COMMITMENT

Although 4-H is probably the least expensive way for your child to obtain excellent instruction in dog care and competitive events, it can be a large and lengthy commitment. 4-H encourages kids to set goals that are both possible and progressive, so as soon as they reach one goal, they begin striving for the next. As kids become quality trainers, they may be asked to help out as junior or teen leaders. Meanwhile, as they advance in dog training, 4-Hers also acquire skills such as leadership, the courage to speak or perform for an audience, and teaching ability. The variety of new challenges keeps kids coming back for more, and it's not unusual for a child to spend five or more productive years in the 4-H program. Naturally, that means a lot of chauffeuring back and forth from meetings and training classes, not to mention listening, offering moral support, and volunteering to help with special projects. Also, in most states, children who win competitive events at the county 4-H fair become eligible to compete at the state fair. Traditionally, this has been a strong incentive for kids to excel in 4-H events; so the better your child does, the bigger your job becomes.

COMMITMENT AND REWARDS

When asked what she thought of her daughter's participation in 4-H, this is what Beth Schroeder had to say about Becky: "I think it's important for any parent who might have a child thinking of becoming involved in the 4-H dog project, showing, or therapy work, to be prepared to make a *huge* commitment of time, money, and emotions. Your level of commitment can dictate your child's level of success. Become responsible pet owners by learning about dog health, nutrition, safety, and the importance of spaying and neutering. Be prepared to spend time with your young person. It's a great opportunity to grow together.

"In looking back over the last six years, I can't think of a single thing I would change. My involvement, through Becky's dog activities, has increased my awareness and love for dogs. I am now an instructor of beginning obedience at a local dog club, and our entire family remains involved with Canine Companions for Independence, a service dog organization dedicated to training dogs for the physically challenged.

"I am extremely proud of what Becky and Saucey have accomplished. It's not the 20 trophies and plaques they've earned, or the bedroom wall covered with ribbons and rosettes, but it's the maturity and grace with which Becky has learned to do things. Respecting the feelings of others, and working as a teen leader helping beginning 4-Hers get started, are just as rewarding as winning awards. So is learning to set goals and following through to their completion. The list goes on and on."

Becky is a 4-H teen leader, has won 4-H events on the state level, earned AKC obedience titles, and raises puppies for a service organization.

VARIETY AND SPICE

Erin Elza, 14, and her sister, Trever, 12, of Royse City, Texas, are active members of the Rockwall County 4-H Dog Project and have placed in obedience, drill team, and conformation at the state level. Their dogs are Canine Good Citizens, and the girls and their dogs march in parades and are part of a dance team that performs at pet shows and SPCA events. (SPCA stands for Society for the Prevention of Cruelty to Animals. There are numerous SPCAs across the country.) Through 4-H, they are raising a puppy for a service dog organization, taking classes in veterinary science, and competing in public speaking (on dog topics, of course). Yet, with all those activities, their 4-H group never loses sight of the most important part—having fun with their dogs.

"At the end of each training session, we play with our dogs," Erin explains. "We run through the park, go in the creek, slide down the slide, go through tunnels and over jumps. We also play with balls and frisbees. Our dogs love training days."

SUPPORTIVE, COMPETITIVE CHAMPIONS

Amy Farkos, of Beecher, Illinois, was 11 years old in 1990 when she fell in love with a little white mixed breed puppy with black spots that was born on a neighboring farm. Even though her mother had already said no, Amy hid the puppy in her jacket and took him home.

"I knew my mother wouldn't be able to send him back once he was in the house," Amy said, "and I was so excited when I got to keep him that I named him Gotcha, because I got him."

Amy's mom encouraged her to enroll Gotcha in the 4-H obedience project, and the puppy was barely a year old when he competed at the county show in 1991. He and Amy thrilled their family by not only winning their class and qualifying for the state championships, but being named county Grand Champions.

There were hundreds of dogs at the state fair, all county qualifiers, so Amy was thrilled when Gotcha took fourth place. By then, Amy's younger sister, Megan, wanted to participate, too. The dog on the neighboring farm had another litter and Megan got Dooley, a half brother to Gotcha.

The following year, Amy and Gotcha won the county Grand Championship again, and Megan and Dooley took first place in the beginner division. Both girls competed at the state fair, with Amy moving up to third place in her class and Megan placing first in beginner competition.

At the county fair in 1993, Amy and Gotcha won first place in their class again and so did Megan and Dooley. But this time, when the county Grand Champions were announced, Megan and Dooley took the honors. At the state fair, both girls won their respective classes, and Amy and Gotcha defeated hundreds of competitors to become the State Champions of Illinois.

Amy and Gotcha repeated their state championship win in 1994, and Megan and Dooley won their class at the county and the state level.

Amy and Megan are looking forward to another year of competition. "I would love to be State Champion for the third year in a row," Amy said, "but Megan has her eye on that trophy as well. My sister and I have been very supportive to each other. We are competing at the same level this year, but I don't go into the ring with the idea of beating her. Instead I think, if I can't win it all, let her!

"The best thing about our dogs," 16-year-old Amy says, "is not how they do in the ring, but that they are great companions and a joy to have around. They go everywhere with us and people never fail to comment on how well behaved they are. Gotcha and Dooley have brought our whole family much joy and love. They even inspired my mother to get involved in the sport of obedience. She now has a two-year-old Border Collie that she works in obedience, agility, and herding."

A WORD FROM THE PARENTS

"We never dreamed what Amy's bringing home a little puppy would lead to," said Kathy Farkos. "We got into all of this quite by accident. I could make an endless list of the positive results, but mainly I feel my daughters have learned responsibility, patience, and a great deal of poise—and don't forget humility.

Megan Farkos praises Dooley for a nice retrieve.

"One of the things I'm most proud of in my children is their kindness and concern toward animals. I think you can tell a lot about a person's character by the way he treats animals. The fact that my children enjoy a working relationship with them is even better!

"One of the most obvious effects of training and practicing is how well Amy and Megan understand the direct relationship between effort and results. They have done all the training, so they know that all the results, both good and bad, are theirs alone.

"Amy and Megan lead somewhat of a different life than most of their friends. With all our animals, they have a lot of responsibility and very little free time. Most of their time is spoken for, but I think this lifestyle has served them well.

"I drive the girls to their weekly classes and pay for them as well as for dog food, vaccinations, and veterinarian bills, and I also vacuum up an awful lot of dog hair every day. But it has always been worth it to me. The opportunity to share a common interest with my daughters is the best part.

"Each August, we look forward to 'girls' week out' at the state fair when Amy and Megan show their dogs. We make a little vacation out of it—just us girls and the dogs—and we have a great time."

As for Mr. Farkos, he says, "The hardest part of my daughters' involvement in 4-H has been having to work other schedules around their training schedules at times. The greatest part is the patience they have developed through working with their animals. Care, understanding, dedication, patience, and love have made the girls and their animals winners."

LEARNING BY DOING

At eight years old, in her first year of 4-H, Natalie Perry of Paulsbo, Washington, created and gave an illustrated presentation to the members of her 4-H group, their parents, and three judges. Rather shy, according to her mother, Natalie worked hard on her talk, as it was a prefair requirement, and she wanted to compete at the fair with her dog. Through this single project, Natalie learned to organize, research, finish before the deadline with enough time to practice, ask for and accept constructive criticism, and perform in public. Natalie says she prepared like this:

"First, I picked my subject. It was Nova Scotia Duck Tolling Retrievers. I chose this subject because my dog, Kit, is a Toller.

"Second, I read about my subject. I read *Quackers*, the Toller newsletter, and articles in *Gun Dog* magazine. I also read about Nova Scotia in the encyclopedia and studied maps.

"Third, I began writing the information I wanted to include in my presentation.

"Fourth, I drew pictures on scratch paper to illustrate the things I wrote about.

"Fifth, I bought a presentation board for five dollars.

"Sixth, I redrew my pictures on big sheets of paper and mounted them in order to my presentation board.

"Then I practiced my speech in front of my 4-H club a few times. One of my club members told me I should call my speech 'A Dog in

Amy Farkos and Gotcha during a demonstration at their county's Frankfort Fest.

Fox Clothing' because he liked the part where I talked about how foxes toll and how people bred Tollers to look like foxes. Other club members also gave me good ideas on how to improve my talk. I was glad I started working on it early. It gave me time to practice and fine-tune things. I was very excited and happy when I received a blue ribbon."

LETTING NATALIE LEARN

Natalie Perry's mother, Caroline Hurst, used to be a 4-H kid, too. These are her feelings on letting children get the most out of the 4-H experience:

"Natalie's first year in 4-H has been very good for her. Her club is large—it has over 20 members ranging in age from 8 (Natalie is the youngest) to 18. I was very happy about this. I remember from my 4-H days that I learned a tremendous amount from the older members in my club. Natalie has already benefited—skill-wise and socially—from sharing her love of dogs with such a diverse group.

"One piece of advice I would like to share with parents looking for a 4-H club is to talk to their veterinarian. Most are quite knowledgeable about local 4-H activities and can help steer people to a good club. Before joining a club, attend a meeting or two as a guest. It's important to (a) assess the dedication, experience, and goals of the leaders and (b) observe the 'climate' and personalities of the other children to make sure the club is a good match.

"Once we found a club we were comfortable with, my husband and I felt the best thing we could do for Natalie was step back and let her participate without a lot of parental advice. We are very supportive and have yet to miss a meeting—but we feel it's important that this be Natalie's activity and not ours. For example, she is responsible for keeping track of meetings and special-event dates and seeing that they are written on the calendar. If she needs to clarify something, she has to call her 4-H leaders or another club member—we won't do it for her. We also try to let her organize her training schedule and time spent on special projects (like her illustrated talk). If she needs special equipment or supplies, we encourage her to earn the money and pay for the items. (Of course we then have to create jobs so she has a way to earn the money.)

Natalie Perry, a member of the Casabapads 4-H club, holds her Nova Scotia Duck Tolling Retriever, Kit. Her brother, Evan, holds his Dachshund, Auggie.

"Natalie was very proud of her illustrated talk. She worked hard, managed her time well, and acted on the suggestions her leaders and club members made during practice sessions. Her blue ribbon was just the frosting on the cake—she already had the satisfaction of knowing she had done well before she ever presented her talk to the judges. Now she's hard at work training her dog for the county fair. She has education matches, fun shows, work parties, a record book to keep current, and many practice sessions between now and then.

"For a child to be truly successful in any activity like 4-H, I think parents need to realize and honor the time commitment required. I'm not just talking about the time spent transporting to and from meetings and events. We also need to be willing to adjust our busy schedules so our children can have uninterrupted blocks of time each week to think, dream, and practice in their own way and at their own pace."

A LASTING LEGACY

Gladys Calderwood of Strongsville, Ohio, has five children, and all of them were 4-H members during the 1960s. Today they are succesful adults (two registered nurses, a nurse technician, an attorney, and an Ohio state trooper), and Gladys believes their 4-H training helped them accomplish their goals. "Their formative years were guided in the right direction by 4-H," she says. "It molded them with the desire to make the best better. Also, their busy lives during childhood produced productive, caring adults who show understanding, patience, kindness, and consideration toward humans and animals."

Kevin Calderwood shows his Siberian Husky at the county fair in 1965. Today he is an Ohio state trooper.

Today, many of Gladys' grandchildren are active 4-H kids.

Chapter 7

The Canine Good Citizen Program

The Canine Good Citizen (CGC) program was created by the American Kennel Club (AKC) to fight antidog legislation and help ensure that dogs will always be welcome in America's cities and towns. At its heart is the belief that all dogs deserve training and care. CGC is a simple training program, culminating with a 10-part, noncompetitive test that evaluates how Cookie responds during simulated everyday situations. If she is calm and mannerly, in good condition, and obeys simple commands, she will pass the test and receive a certificate proclaiming her a Canine Good Citizen.

Lena Condrashoff, 12, and her dog, Grumpy, 10, of Concord, California, proudly display their Canine Good Citizen certificate.

The Canine Good Citizen program is available to all dogs (purebred or mixed) and all handlers (whether or not they attend organized classes). A relatively short and inexpensive commitment, CGC gives you an opportunity to see if David really does enjoy dog training and will stick with it until he proudly hangs Cookie's certificate on the wall.

Earning a CGC certificate can be either a goal in itself or an excellent starting point, leading to further training in another activity. Since

CGC training is universal, like teaching a child how to read, a CGC background gives Cookie an advantage when going into any other field. Best of all, Canine Good Citizens are lovely to live with and a pleasure in public places.

WHAT MAKES A CANINE GOOD CITIZEN?

The American Kennel Club defines a Canine Good Citizen as "a dog that makes its owner happy, without making someone else unhappy." In short, a Canine Good Citizen is a dog who has been taught to behave in everyday social situations, such as sitting in the veterinarian's waiting room or being petted by a friendly stranger when out for a walk.

A Canine Good Citizen is a dog who has been taught to behave in everyday social situations.

In order to become a Canine Good Citizen, Cookie must pass every part of the 10-part test. Each part is scored on a pass-fail basis, and dogs that do not pass on the first try are eligible to be tested again after further training. However, they must repeat every part of the test, not just the section they failed.

The test itself is informal and fun. The evaluators are usually helpful, and will cheerfully answer David's questions before testing begins. David will be allowed to talk to Cookie throughout the test and may use more than one command whenever necessary. But he will not be allowed to yell at Cookie or use his hands to force her into the correct position.

THE 10-PART TEST

A dog has to be legal in its community before it can be acclaimed a good citizen. So, before testing begins, David will have to show proof of Cookie's rabies vaccination and any other licenses required in his locale.

Test 1. During Test 1, which is called Accepting a Friendly Stranger, the evaluator will walk up to David and Cookie and the two people will greet each other and shake hands while ignoring Cookie. Cookie will pass this test if she shows no resentment or shyness and doesn't try to touch the evaluator. This scenario takes into account that overly exuberant, friendly dogs can be a problem, too. Dogs who pass this test wouldn't rip a woman's panty hose by jumping up on her in glee, or tangle their leash around a senior citizen's legs.

Test 2. Strangers often ask permission to pet a dog, and that's what Test 2, Sitting Politely for Petting, anticipates. During this test, David will tell Cookie to sit and the evaluator will walk over and pet Cookie on the head and body. Then the evaluator will circle David and Cookie to make sure Cookie isn't afraid or angry when a friendly stranger is behind her.

Test 3. Test 3 is called Appearance and Grooming. Now the evaluator will check Cookie for cleanliness and condition, brush her, examine her ears, and pick up each of her front feet. Passing the test demonstrates that David maintains Cookie in reasonably healthy condition and that Cookie will permit a stranger, such as a veterinarian or groomer, to handle her.

Test 4. Test 4 is called Out for a Walk, and it demonstrates that David is in control. During the test, David may talk to Cookie in a cheerful manner just as if they were enjoying a walk in the neighborhood. Cookie may walk on either side of David on a loose leash, but does not have to be in the formal heel position used in competitive obedience work. The evaluator will tell David when to turn and where to stop, and he and Cookie should move together smoothly, without either one pulling on the leash. When David stops, Cookie should stop too, but she does not have to sit as she would at an obedience trial.

Test 5. Cookie will go Walking Through a Crowd on Test 5, by moving around or through a group of at least three people. She may show interest in the people but not fear or resentment, and she must not strain against the leash. Passing this test shows that she remembers her manners in public places.

Test 6. Test 6, Sit and Down on Command and Staying in Place, evaluates Cookie's response to simple commands, including remaining in place when told. Prior to the test, the leash will be replaced by a 20-foot line. When the test begins, David will be asked to demonstrate that Cookie obeys his commands to sit and down. After that, David may choose to leave Cookie in either the sit or the down position, give a stay command, and walk to the end of the long line. The exercise ends when David returns to Cookie. To pass, Cookie must remain where David left her, but she may change position.

Your dog will be required to obey the sit and down commands as part of the Canine Good Citizen test.

Test 7. Test 7 is called Coming When Called, and its purpose is to prove that Cookie will do just that. With Cookie in a sit position, David will walk 10 feet away, then turn to face Cookie and call her to him. David is allowed to use body language and encouragement when calling Cookie. Cookie should respond positively and promptly.

Test 8. Test 8 evaluates Cookie's Reaction to Another Dog. David and Cookie will approach another dog and handler team, and both handlers will speak and shake hands. Cookie and the strange dog may show a casual interest in each other, but neither dog should approach the other dog or handler. Passing this test demonstrates that Cookie behaves in the presence of other dogs.

Test 9. Cookie's Reaction to Distractions will be evaluated through Test 9. During this test, she may show natural curiosity and may even startle at the sight or the sound, but she should not panic, become aggressive, or bark. The CGC program booklet lists eight types of normal, everyday distractions, such as someone wheeling a shopping cart or dropping a large book. Two of these designated distractions will be used at the actual test, so don't encourage David to invent scary scenarios to test Cookie's reaction. The object of this test is to see how Cookie reacts to everyday incidents, not to frighten her.

Test 10. The final test, Supervised Separation, evaluates separation anxiety by having David hand Cookie's leash to the evaluator and go to a place out of her sight for three minutes. This is not a stay exercise, so Cookie may stand, sit, lie down, and change positions during the test. Mild worry or slight nervousness is okay, but Cookie will not pass if she continually barks, whines, howls, paces, or tries to break loose. Passing this test shows that she can be left with someone else in an emergency without it causing her undue stress.

That's all there is to earning the Canine Good Citizen certificate. The 10 tests demonstrate that Cookie is a mannerly, reliable best friend.

PREPARING FOR THE CGC CHALLENGE

David can prepare for the Canine Good Citizen test by attending beginner training classes at a dog-club-sponsored or privately owned training school (some schools offer the test as the graduation exam), or he can use the techniques in AKC's program booklet to teach Cookie the correct responses on his own.

If David has never trained a dog before, and Cookie had no previous training, organized classes would be best for both of them. Kids training alone are often impatient, beginning new exercises before perfecting the previous ones. An instructor makes sure a good foundation is laid before moving on, and corrects training mistakes before they become bad habits.

Being part of a group also makes training more interesting, as class situations usually include both teamwork and a touch of competition. As for Cookie, she will be expected to take the test in the company of strangers and other dogs, so classes will help her learn to respond properly, despite distractions.

Cookie should be able to do all 10 exercises in the company of other people and other manageable dogs before she is tested. But she should never be forced to endure the playful teasing or bullying of an untrained and unleashed dog while she is practicing.

The American Kennel Club provides information on how to prepare a dog for the Canine Good Citizen test, so if David can't attend training classes, he can follow the flyer and go it alone. To receive CGC training information, or to find a club near you that offers CGC testing to the public, write to the American Kennel Club (the address is given in appendix 1).

If David attempts CGC training on his own, give him encouragement every small step of the way and remind him that dogs learn through praise and repetition. For Cookie's sake, David should practice no more than 10 to 15 minutes once or twice a day, and repeat each lesson many times over a period of several days. It's important that he praise every correct response and that Cookie knows her role well before they move on to the next lesson.

If David trains Cookie so well that she earns her Canine Good Citizen certificate, he has proven both his dedication and her ability. This pair deserves an opportunity to advance into activities such as obedience, agility, tracking, animal-assisted therapy, or breed-specific sporting events.

Chapter 8

Obedience

O bedience could be called "companion-dog training," as it teaches the dog to be a pleasant and responsive partner, while teaching the handler how to train, enjoy, and understand the dog. The result is enhanced companionship. Obedience buffs often say "a trained dog is a happy dog," and they are right. Trained dogs are a pleasure and consequently are taken on more outings, are welcome in more places, and generally enjoy a fuller life. Earning titles and winning awards are great, but the ultimate goal of every trainer should be a happy working dog with a trustworthy temperament.

A sport that demonstrates the dog's many talents, obedience training is an exciting endeavor with enough major challenges and frequent rewards to keep Michelle and Prince active and occupied. While

Jessica Newell of Saranac, Michigan, practices the Stand for Examination exercise with her Shetland Sheepdog, Topper. Jessica is eight years old.

Cassie Jackson, 14, says her family didn't know what they got themselves into when they adopted rambunctious, 10-month-old Spike from the Humane Society. He was big, smart, and energetic, and the family soon realized that he was badly in need of training.

"Spike and I enrolled in a 10-week beginners course," Cassie said, "and with 15 minutes practice a day and a lot of hard work and patience, I learned how to direct Spike's intelligence. He graduated first in our class."

After the beginner course, Cassie and Spike flew through a progressive intermediate course in five weeks instead of the usual ten. Now they are perfecting the novice exercises, and Spike already earned

Cassie Jackson, of Minneapolis, Minnesota, and her well-trained partner, Spike.

the first leg toward his CD title with AMBOR. But doing well in competition is secondary to Cassie. She has already achieved her goal of turning a difficult dog into a best friend.

"My friends are always impressed when I give Spike his down hand signal and he responds without question," Cassie said. "And I'm still amazed when I think about taking 89 pounds of raw dog and turning him into a polite family member."

teaching Prince the obedience exercises, Michelle will learn training skills, goal setting, problem solving, perseverance, and teamwork. After the exercises are perfected, competing in trials will teach her to practice sportsmanship, think on her feet, and remain composed while performing for an audience.

Available to all dogs, purebred or mixed, obedience is comprised of established exercises of varying difficulty. Each exercise is actually a combination of several trained responses, short-term goals that are each perfected individually then combined to make up the finished exercise. While competing in obedience trials is a comprehensive sport all by itself, obedience training is valuable even if Prince never attends a competitive event. It is also a vital first step on the way to preparing for other activities, such as agility, hunting tests, or animal-assisted therapy.

Obedience titles are awarded at three levels of difficulty, and earning even the first title takes a moderate to heavy commitment. Michelle and Prince will need tuition and transportation to obedience classes. They may also join an obedience club for the opportunity to practice with other trainers and their dogs. This entails paying dues (usually reasonable) and attending practice sessions and meetings. When they are ready to compete in obedience trials, there will be entry fees to pay and transportation to provide, and the trials may be some distance from home. With luck, Michelle and Prince will have an opportunity to test their skills at practice trials (called matches) before finding themselves amid the bustle of a real obedience trial. Entry fees at matches are inexpensive, and matches are excellent preparation for official competitions.

OBEDIENCE TRIALS

Obedience trials are offered by the American Kennel Club (AKC), the United Kennel Club (UKC), the American Mixed Breed Obedience Registry (AMBOR), and various other organizations. They may be held indoors or outside in all kinds of weather.

One of the basic obedience exercises is heeling on a loose lead. Here Meghann Phillips practices with her dog, Cody. Meghann belongs to the Working Paws 4-H group and lives in Saranac, New York.

When competing at the novice level, Michelle and Prince will perform exercises individually as well as in a group with other dogs and handlers. They will be judged by one judge via a score sheet, and will begin with a perfect score of 200. Each exercise is worth a prescribed number of points if performed perfectly, and the judge deducts points for every mistake.

To qualify (pass) and earn one leg toward a Companion Dog title, Michelle and Prince will have to finish with scores of more than 50 percent of the available points in each exercise, and a grand total of 170 or more points. Michelle will receive a ribbon every time Prince qualifies. Obtaining qualifying scores under three different judges earns Prince the title of Companion Dog (AKC's or AMBOR's CD or UKC's U-CD). He will receive a certificate from the registry and the title will become an official part of his registered name.

Winners of first through fourth place are also announced at obedience trials and receive ribbons and sometimes trophies. Winning a placement takes a higher degree of precision and teamwork than simply qualifying. While many handlers relish the challenge, others lack the time or inclination for intense training and are happy to obtain a qualifying score.

Michelle should be encouraged to set a personal goal for herself and Prince. A realistic goal takes into consideration her handling experience and ability, Prince's competitive potential, and how much time they can devote to achieving nearly perfect performances. Depending on these factors, feasible goals range from simply passing the exercises and earning an obedience title (a considerable job in itself), to bettering their own score each time they compete, to trying to win their class.

COMPANION DOG EXERCISES

The AKC's and AMBOR's Companion Dog (CD) title involves six exercises. The first one is the Heel on Leash and Figure Eight. This exercise demonstrates Michelle and Prince's ability to work as a team. Prince will be required to move along with Michelle in heel position (close to Michelle's left side but not so close as to interfere with her movements) on a loose lead. The judge will call out orders such as "Forward," "Right turn," "Left turn," "About turn," "Slow," "Fast," and "Halt," and Prince will remain in heel position as Michelle follows the judge's commands. Every time Michelle halts, Prince will automatically sit at her left side.

During the Figure Eight, two people (called ring stewards) will stand eight feet apart and Michelle and Prince will walk completely around and between each of them two times. The judge will call at least one halt during the exercise and another at the end.

Michelle and Prince should pass both parts of the first exercise if Michelle handles Prince on a loose lead and Prince is attentive to Michelle's commands, changes speed and direction with her, and stays close to heel position. Prince will lose points for such faults as heeling too far from Michelle, interfering with her movements, failing to sit when she stops, not changing pace on the fast or the slow, lagging behind, or forging ahead. Michelle will lose points for mistakes such as holding the leash too tight, giving extra commands (only one command is allowed per exercise), and adapting her pace to Prince instead

"Training and showing Peppy has had a big influence on my life," says Darcie Peterson, 14, of Ophiem, Illinois. "I've made many new friends in many different cities. My success with Peppy in obedience has greatly increased my self-confidence. Peppy has taken me places I never would have gone without him. He is my best friend, listens to all my problems and secrets, and is always there when I need him. Life without a dog—never!"

Darcie's twin brother, Dustin, chimes in: "I'm not always as consistent in training as Darcie, but I do enjoy it. Playing baseball makes my summer a little more hectic than hers. I don't know if I will keep training dogs forever, as I'm sure Darcie will, but I have learned a lot from my experiences with Nikki. Even if I stop training and showing dogs, I'm sure that I will always have a dog in my life."

Their mother, Sharon, says, "In a world where so many bad things are happening to kids, dog obedience and 4-H are activities that require both time and effort. The kids learn values that will stay with them all their lives. They also don't have the extra time to become involved in just 'hanging out' or become part of a 'bad' group of kids."

Dustin and Darcie Peterson, 14-year-old twins from Ophiem, Illinois, have each trained and handled their own dog at AKC obedience trials. Dustin and his Sheltie, Nikki (a rescue dog), have earned a CD, and Darcie put a CDX on Peppy the Papillon.

Fourteen-year-old Carrie Walton leads her Shetland Sheepdog, Tara, around one of the "posts" in the off-lead Figure Eight exercise. Tara has earned a CDX title, her CGC title, and she's a registered Therapy Dog.

of training him to keep up with her. It's possible to lose several points and still pass the exercise.

The second exercise is the Stand for Examination. Before scoring begins, Michelle will remove the leash and hand it to a steward. Then the judge will indicate an area of the ring and tell Michelle to stand Prince there and leave when she is ready. Michelle may use any gentle method she wants to position Prince into a stand, and should take her time and make certain he is steady before giving the stay command. Then she should walk six feet in front of Prince and turn to face him while the judge touches the dog's head and strokes his back. When the judge tells Michelle to go back to her dog, she should return by walking behind Prince to reach heel position.

Prince will pass this exercise if he receives only one command, stays in position before and during the judge's examination, and does not show any resentment. Minor points are lost for mistakes such as slight movement of the feet during the examination or sitting down following the examination.

The exercise called Heel Free or Heel Off Leash is next. It follows the same pattern as the on-leash heeling exercise but does not include the figure eight.

The Recall exercise is composed of three parts. Before judging begins, Michelle will go to the end of the ring indicated by the judge and have Prince sit beside her in heel position. Scoring begins when the judge tells Michelle to leave Prince. At that time, Michelle will give the stay command, walk to the other end of the ring, and turn to face her dog. Then, on the judge's signal, Michelle will call Prince. Ideally, Prince will respond immediately, hurry to Michelle, and sit in front of her, facing her. The judge's last command will be "Finish," and Michelle will send Prince back to heel position.

Michelle and Prince will pass this exercise if Michelle gives only three commands: one for stay, one for come, and one for finish. Prince will pass if he stays in place until Michelle calls him, comes when called, and stops close enough to Michelle so that she could touch his head without moving or stretching. Points are lost for faults such as coming in slowly, sitting crookedly instead of directly in front of the Michelle, and performing a sloppy finish or no finish at all. Michelle and Prince will leave the ring following the Recall exercise but will return later, along with other handlers and dogs, for the Long Sit and the Long Down.

THE GROUP EXERCISES

The Long Sit and the Long Down are performed in a line with other dogs, and unless Prince happens to be assigned an end position, there will be a dog on either side of him. Michelle will walk Prince into the ring on leash and position him in his place in the line. Then she will remove the leash and her arm band and place both of them behind Prince with the arm band number facing the judge. Although Prince should be sitting by Michelle's side in heel position when the judge gives the command "Sit your dogs," she should give the sit command anyway as a reminder. When the judge says "Leave your dogs," all the handlers will give the stay signal and command in unison, walk to the other end of the ring, and turn to face their dogs. After one minute the judge will command "Back to your dogs," and the handlers will return and walk around behind their dogs to heel position. When all the handlers are standing beside their dogs, the judge will say "Exercise finished."

The Long Down is the final exercise. It begins when the judge says "Down your dogs," and is performed exactly like the Long Sit except that the dogs must remain down for three minutes.

Prince will pass the group exercises if he sits and downs on command and remains in position and in place, without whining or barking, until Michelle returns. He will lose points for mistakes such as whining or barking even once, moving a little bit, or changing position just as Michelle returns (before the judge says the exercise is finished).

"I had been campaigning for a dog for many years when my parents finally gave in," says 14-year-old Kate Anders of Minneapolis, Minnesota. "At the time, we knew nothing about dog obedience, but we agreed that the dog would be my responsibility and I would be the sole owner and care giver.

"My father works with a woman who trains her dogs for obedience trials, and she insisted that if my parents got me a dog, I had to train it. Shortly after that, I accompanied her to Animal Inn Training School, where I observed an open class. Because I had never seen a dog heel, retrieve a dumbbell, or jump a broad jump, I was amazed. The instructor, Sharon Anderson (who would become my teacher), explained that it would take a long time and a lot of hard work before my dog would be jumping or retrieving. I went home that night bubbling with excitement.

"My dad knew someone who had a litter of puppies, and two weeks later I found myself driving home holding the puppy of my dreams. We attended puppy kindergarten together, and moved up from there. Because Charlotte is a mix, we joined AMBOR, and earned a CD. We are currently in Open, working on the same jumps I never thought my dog could possibly do.

"I have found three really hard parts of dog obedience training. The hardest is being patient. As a youth, I'm just

Kate Anders and her Golden Retriever/Setter mix, Charlotte. The team won an AMBOR award for highest scoring junior handler while earning the CD title.

beginning to believe that changes don't happen overnight. The second difficulty is transportation. In a few months I will be able to drive, but until then I have to drag a parent everywhere I want to go. Both of my parents are very busy, and even an hour a week is a lot. The third problem is the cold, snowy Minnesota winter, which makes it hard to train outside. This is especially a problem now that Charlotte is jumping.

"The best part of training is not the pride I feel when Charlotte does well in a show and it's not the satisfaction I feel when Charlotte comes bounding toward me with just one command. The real reason I love training is because with every new thing Charlotte learns to do, she changes just a little. After each training session, Charlotte seems to hold her head higher, knowing she has done something worthwhile. Now to most people, a straight sit or a fast drop on recall doesn't mean much, but to us, it's some kind of perfection."

Rudi Anders, Kate's father, comments: "My great fear, probably like that of many other parents, was that Kate would be happy with a puppy but would soon tire of the responsibilities entailed in caring for a dog. On the one hand, I wanted Kate to learn to take care of something that needed more attention than a cat or a gerbil. On the other hand, we did not wish to be stuck taking care of another animal.

"Ultimately the dog-training classes did more than my wife or I to convince Kate of the importance of training her dog. I've always joked that I wish I had gone to those classes prior to the birth of my children—one quick correction on a leash. Kidding aside, the basics apply in either case: being consistent with a dog or a child and communicating your desires as clearly as possible. Kate's success with Charlotte is of her own making."

UKC—SIMILAR BUT DIFFERENT

The UKC Companion Dog (U-CD) exercises are quite similar, with two exceptions. Instead of a Long Down, there is an exercise called Honoring. A dog honors by remaining in the down position, alone and off leash, with its handler facing it from across the ring, while another dog performs the Heel on Leash and Figure Eight exercise nearby. Prince will pass the Honoring exercise if he remains in place and in position and does not whine or bark. He will lose points but will still qualify on this exercise if he moves slightly or sits up just as Michelle returns.

The U-CD Recall is the same as the AKC Recall except that it includes a high jump with a steward standing on each side of it. Prince will pass this exercise if he stays in position until called, comes immediately when called, jumps the jump on the way in, and sits within an arm's length of Michelle. He will lose minor points for such faults as sitting crooked and not performing a precise finish.

ADVANCED TITLES

After Michelle and Prince earn their CD, U-CD, or both (many registered purebreds compete in AKC and UKC events, and mixed breeds registered with AMBOR may also compete for UKC titles), Michelle may want to continue training Prince for advanced work. Whether or not she will be able to do so depends, to a large degree, on Prince's age and potential.

Advanced goals include AKC's and AMBOR's Companion Dog Excellent (CDX) and Utility Dog (UD), and UKC's Companion Dog Excellent (U-CDX) and Utility Dog (U-UD) titles. CDX and U-CDX exercises encompass work such as high jumps, broad jumps, downing in the midst of a recall, retrieving both from the ground and over jumps, and staying in place with the handler out of sight.

UD and U-UD work includes a signal exercise (heeling and obeying various hand signals without verbal commands), scent discrimination (finding and retrieving the article their handler touched from among several articles), a directed retrieve (retrieving the article they were directed to from among three choices), and directed jumping (a complicated three-part exercise that culminates when the dog responds to its handler's signal telling it which of two jumps to return over).

AKC and AMBOR also award a UDX title to dogs that earn 10 additional qualifying scores at the Utility level after earning the UD. Most competitive of all is the Obedience Trial Champion title. It is earned by accumulating 100 points for defeating other dogs at the CDX and UD levels.

GETTING STARTED

While almost any healthy dog of any breed or body type is capable of earning a Companion Dog title, the advanced titles require a moderately agile dog because jumping is featured in several exercises. With competitive obedience in mind, many handlers carefully select their

Darcie Peterson's Papillon, Peppy, comes leaping over the high jump while practicing the advanced exercise of Directed Jumping.

dogs from a few breeds especially known for excelling in the sport, such as the Golden Retriever, the Shetland Sheepdog, and the Border Collie. After carefully testing many puppies for obedience potential, they bring their chosen one home when it is seven weeks old and begin preparing for its future. Preparations include thorough socialization (taking the puppy many places so it learns to be confident in all situations) and Kindergarten Puppy Classes, where it learns to get along with other puppies and enjoy people of all ages.

Assuming that Prince was already a member of your family when Michelle decided to train him for obedience, it may or may not be fair to expect him to earn advanced titles. If he is under five years old, active, and enjoyed Companion Dog training, he is probably a good candidate for further obedience work. But if he is older than five, and prefers sleeping to playing, advanced training could be a difficult chore for handler and dog. More suitable activities also offer exciting possibilities. For example, healthy dogs of all ages and activity levels can learn tracking, and obedience-trained dogs are especially valued in animal-assisted therapy.

LEARNING THE BASICS

Michelle should get her basic instruction in a class rather than by private lessons. When choosing an instructor, be certain to select one who will teach her how to handle Prince, not one who will train the dog for her and then show her the signals that make him perform. For Michelle to understand fully how to train her dog and enforce the training, she should be the trainer, not just the handler. Doing it herself will not only give her the greatest satisfaction, but will assure her of being able to train the dogs she owns later in life.

Most young handlers respond best to instructors who talk to them on an adult level and have equally high expectations for all their students, regardless of age. Competent instructors also make the goals clear, and their lesson plans work progressively toward them.

Anyone can simply call out commands, but excellent teachers have patience and a sense of humor, provide answers to any training situation, and take the time to solve individual problems. There are several ways to teach every obedience exercise, and resourceful instructors know when and how to switch procedures if the first method isn't doing the job. They also use creativity when drilling the exercises, instead of simply repeating the same commands over and over. If Michelle's goal is competitive obedience, she will need an instructor who has successfully handled dogs at obedience trials and has coached students who have earned titles.

There are many obedience clubs across the country, and most of them offer quality training classes for new handlers as well as practice sessions for club members. Depending on where Prince is registered, contact AKC, UKC, or AMBOR (appendix 1) for a list of their obedience clubs and a copy of their obedience rules. Michelle should read the sections of the rules pertaining to exhibitors before entering her first trial.

Private obedience instructors may be found in the yellow pages of the phone book or the classified section of the newspaper. Many of them are excellent, as their professional reputations depend upon their ability to turn their students into winning exhibitors.

ENTERING TRIALS

Magazines published by AKC, UKC, and AMBOR (appendix 2) list when and where obedience trials will be held, and your local obedience club will also have information about trials in your area. Some obedience trials will be in conjunction with dog shows, and others stand alone. They are so popular that several trials are held in various parts of the country practically every weekend of the year, and Michelle may not have to travel very far to earn a Companion Dog title.

Entries to AKC events must be made in advance, most often through a show superintendent. Several months before she plans to compete in AKC trials, Michelle should send a postcard with her name

"Saucey is a little dog with a big heart," says her owner and trainer, 15-year-old Becky Schroeder of Kalamazoo, Michigan.

Indeed, Becky and her Shetland Sheepdog, Saucey, have earned their CDX title three times—at AKC, UKC, and Canadian Kennel Club (CKC) shows, and have more than 20 trophies and plaques, a wall full of ribbons, and numerous Best Junior Handler awards from obedience trials. Becky planned to continue their winning ways and trained Saucey for the highest level, utility. Then she changed her mind.

Becky Schroeder and Saucey, CDX, U-CDX, and Canadian CDX, get ready for the Figure Eight exercise at UKC's Top Gun competition.

"Saucey developed progressing cataracts and I noticed some change in her judgment when jumping and decided to retire her from the show ring," Becky says. "Obedience titles don't mean anything to me if I jeopardize her well-being. I know she would do whatever I asked, but I don't want to see her get hurt just to win a ribbon. Saucey is my best friend and we enjoy each other's company, and you don't have to be a show dog to do that."

and address to each show superintendent listed in the back of this book and request to be put on the mailing list for Obedience trials.

If Prince is a rare breed that is registered in some other country but not recognized by the AKC, contact the UKC. They register many rare breeds and may welcome Prince.

Kids must enter their dogs in obedience trials in advance, but it's not hard to find one—they're so popular they're held almost every weekend all over the country.

If Prince is a mixed breed, registry in AMBOR makes him eligible to compete in AMBOR and UKC obedience. Contact AMBOR (appendix 1) for an information packet and an enrollment form.

Whether Michelle chooses to learn the basics of obedience training so Prince will be a better companion, or decides to compete in trials, her experience with this sport, and its demands of goal setting, poise, practice, and patience, will help her in the years ahead.

Chapter 9

Animal-Assisted Therapy Volunteer

I t's a scientific fact that interacting with animals is therapeutic for humans. That's why hundreds of dog owners warm aging hearts and thrill disabled children by visiting institutions with their affectionate, well-mannered dogs. Some choose one facility—a senior citizens' home, for example—and make weekly or biweekly visits on a regular schedule. Others join one of the hundreds of therapy clubs across the nation.

These dedicated groups visit a variety of local institutions and hospitals, inviting the residents to pet and play with their dogs. The results are always positive, and occasionally they are astonishing. There are documented cases of minor miracles, where patients who hadn't spoken a word in years talked to the lovable dog snuggling in their lap, and withdrawn children laughed gleefully as they played ball with their gentle new friend. While Sue may not witness miracles while performing pet therapy, she will surely bring a bit of sunshine to brighten drab, often pain-filled lives.

All dogs, purebred or mixed, are welcome in pet-assisted therapy programs. Requirements vary from one therapy-dog organization to another and sometimes from institution to institution, but generally the dog will have to pass one or more tests before being allowed to participate.

Tests for therapy dogs evaluate both temperament and training because it's vital that the dogs have dependable

Carrie Walton, 15, and her costumed therapy dogs, Misty and Tara, performed at an Easter childrens' benefit at FAO Schwarz toy store in San Francisco.

dispositions and impeccable manners. They must also obey basic commands while surrounded by service equipment (wheelchairs and walkers, for example), institutional odors, crowds, and noise.

Perhaps the test most frequently used to certify dogs for therapy work is AKC's Canine Good Citizen (CGC) test (explained in detail in chapter 7). Therapy Dog International (TDI), a pet-facilitated therapy organization, uses the basic CGC test, with modifications to simulate people using service equipment. Dogs accepted by TDI are privileged to wear a yellow TDI tag on their collars, and their owners receive an identification card. There are TDI chapters in most major cities and many towns.

"Topper loves to visit, and I think it's fun to make the people happy," says Jessica Newell, 8, of Saranac, Michigan. Jessica is a member of the Working Paws 4-H Club, and one of their activities is visiting nursing homes.

GETTING STARTED IN ANIMAL-ASSISTED THERAPY

In addition to Therapy Dogs International, numerous other organizations feature animal-assisted therapy. For example, the Delta Society's Pet Partners Program encourages youth participation and provides training for human volunteers and screening for animals. Volunteers are thoroughly educated by Delta's certified instructors, in cooperation with humane and veterinary organizations, breed clubs, and health care facilities.

If Delta has no workshops near your home, Sue can educate herself through the Pet Partners Home Study Course. The course consists of articles and a videotape with all the practical information volunteers need to become successful Pet Partners. To be eligible for Delta's program, Sue must be 10 years of age or older and be able to complete all the registration materials.

Sparky's certification through Delta begins with a visit to a Pet Partners animal evaluator, who gives a skills and aptitude evaluation. Then Sparky will have to pass additional tests administered by a veterinarian, and a complete health examination. After Sparky passes his tests, and Sue completes the educational program, they will receive a pet tag, a volunteer identification card, and a subscription to the Pet Partners newsletter. Delta's Youth or Student registration fee is $25 for two years.

Young Pet Partners plan their visitations in a variety of ways. Some are part of a group, such as a 4-H project or a dog club. Others contact an institution on their own, explain their credentials as Delta Pet Partners, and volunteer their services.

Delta divides the work of animals in institutions into two classifications: Animal-Assisted Activities (AAA) and Animal-Assisted Therapy (AAT). AAA volunteers visit informally with hospital patients, nursing home residents, and people in various types of institutions. AAT programs are more demanding. Volunteers and their pets work

The Chapman sisters, Rebekah, 10, Beth, 16, and Anna, 13, of Angora, Minnesota, are active members of the 4-H club, Paw Partners, with their dogs, Dozer, Oreo, and Patches. Anna teaches junior showmanship and Beth teaches obedience, and their dogs have earned Canine Good Citizen certificates. In addition to participating in parades, animal-assisted therapy, and frequent demos, the girls' 4-H club was involved in project Bite Awareness. They went to schools and taught children how to properly approach a friendly dog and avoid an aggressive one.

Therapy dogs and handlers don't have to wear costumes, but sometimes they can add to the fun. The frog and lily pad are Becky Schroeder and her therapy dog, Saucey.

Becky Schroeder is a 15-year-old from Kalamazoo, Michigan, who volunteers with her dogs. She says, "Through my involvement with VolunTEEN, I got involved with their pet-therapy program. Saucey soon became a favorite visitor for many of the residents and I learned a lot about the elderly and just what an important role pets still play in their lives. One resident who was verbally abusive and occasionally physically violent became very calm and loving when Saucey was held where he could pet her and kiss her. The observing nurses actually cried when Walter said 'Thank You,' instead of his usual four-letter word. From then on, Saucey became known as 'Walter's dog.'

Becky's mother, Beth, says, "Involvement in pet therapy is a very rewarding experience. Many young people today have no idea how to relate to and talk to our senior citizens. Through visiting a local nursing home, Becky has been given the opportunity to become comfortable with older people. She talks to them easily and has seen numerous times how important dogs can be to people at this stage in their lives. It also put us in touch with the fact that death is part of life, as we've lost many of our friends at the nursing home over time. It's comforting to know that visiting with our dogs brightened their day a little."

with therapists and become formally involved in patient treatment on a regular schedule. Young people and most adult volunteers participate in AAA work, but older teens with AAA experience sometimes work toward AAT goals, such as learning the special skills necessary to help people recover from strokes or head injuries. Volunteers who want advanced training may attend Delta's seminars on how to train a therapy dog.

To contact TDI, the Delta Society, and other animal-assisted therapy groups, see appendix 1.

ADDITIONAL POSSIBILITIES IN PET THERAPY

A variety of dog clubs also train and supply volunteers for animal-assisted therapy. To find therapy clubs in your area, call local institutions such as nursing homes and children's hospitals. Ask if they host pet-therapy groups and how such groups can be contacted.

Some institutions have their own requirements, and even hold graduation ceremonies for pet-therapy trainees who qualify to become volunteers. For example, a nursing home in New York state has a program especially geared to its needs, complete with a detailed manual and stringent requirements.

To qualify for its program, dogs must pass the therapy version of the Canine Good Citizen test and undergo a thorough veterinary examination, including stools and blood. Then they attend four training sessions at the nursing home to become familiar with crowded elevators, slippery floors, and the sights and smells of the institution. During these sessions, they also work with willing patients; first one-on-one, then in small groups of two or three patients to a dog, and finally the maximum of six patients at a time.

While the dogs learn, they are evaluated by the staff. Dog and handler teams that have the training and temperament for the work are invited to serve internships of six visits within three months. Evaluation continues during each visitation, and if all goes well, they are invited to a graduation ceremony and permitted to sign up for regular visits.

THE PARENT'S ROLE

After training and testing is complete, and Sue and Sparky are official pet-therapy volunteers, the financial commitment is low to moderate and the amount of time and travel will depend on how frequently they serve. If Sue is too young to drive, she will need transportation to and from the institutions. Also, if she is under driving age, it would be best if one parent (or both) accompanied her during her visits, unless she is with a group of animal-assisted volunteers. Costs include paying for the complete veterinary examination for Sparky, and paying training, testing, and registration fees in a therapy organization.

Providing moral support is a parent's most important role. Through her volunteer work, Sue may have her first personal encounter with children suffering from terminal diseases. She may also interact with the mentally and physically handicapped and witness the difficulties of advanced age. It's a good idea to prepare Sue for what she might see and feel before she visits a new institution, and, when the visit is over, make time to listen because she may need to talk.

"I think therapy work is good for the dogs, the people who handle them and the people they visit," says 11-year-old Lia Temarantz of Wilkes-Barre, Pennsylvania. "Even though I'm in the sixth grade and have a lot of homework and projects to do, I manage my time so I can fit in other things like therapy work and dog training."

Barbara Ann Temarantz, mother of Lia and her younger sister, Ami, responds: "I can't sing enough praises about therapy-dog work. Not only is one's canine companion shared, but also one's self. The girls deal easily with the elderly as well as the infirm or impaired. The interaction is special and unique, and everyone benefits from the time each spends with the other."

Ami and Lia Temarantz and their therapy dogs, Scarlet and Tootsie (the Lhasa Apsos) and Rachel (the Poodle), get ready to march in the Bethlehem, Pennsylvania, Halloween parade.

MAGIC MOMENTS

Miracles or not, there is always magic in animal-assisted therapy, especially when offered by a young person and his or her dog. Although Sparky will be the focus of attention during the visits, the combination of a dog and a young handler may encourage a painfully shy child to join in a petting session, or bring a laugh to the lips of a depressed oldster. If Sue feels anxious about her ability to interact with

Jessica Newell and Topper during a nursing home visit. Jessica is a second-generation 4-H club member. Her mother also learned about dogs through 4-H and is a dog project leader.

her audience, remind her that Sparky is the one giving the therapy, and she is simply making it possible by sharing him with those in need. When she sees bored eyes light up and mouths pinched with pain relax into smiles, she will understand that she and Sparky are giving a great gift and receiving wondrous rewards just by being there.

Chapter 10

Agility

Agility is the doggie version of a challenging obstacle course. The epitome of exciting teamwork between handler and dog, this stirring sport blends desire, control, and athletic ability into a rip-roaring good time. In fact, agility is sometimes referred to as the sport for everyone since it's fun for the dogs, their handlers, and the cheering spectators. Best of all, it's available to every dog, pure-bred or mixed (except AKC agility, which is available only to AKC-registered dogs).

At agility trials, dogs crawl through brightly decorated tunnels, maneuver seesaws, stride across balance beams, sprint up A-frames, and soar over creatively shaped jumps. And they do it all at high speed while taking direction from their handlers. Big dogs don't have an advantage over little dogs either. There are height divisions at agility trials, and the height of the jump will be adjusted for Buck's size.

Jamie Watters, 14, of Hudson, Wisconsin, works the agility course teeter-totter with her Border Collie, Annie.

To prepare for agility trials, Carl will teach Buck how to navigate each type of obstacle. This slow, step-by-step process must be communicated with a consistently upbeat attitude and much praise. Besides learning patience, training Buck for agility trials will teach Carl how to break down large problems into small, solvable parts. Soon he will be able to study an obstacle, divide it into simple components, and teach them to Buck one step at a time. Finally, after Buck perfects each individual section, Carl will put the parts together and work on mastering the whole obstacle.

REWARDS AND AWARDS

One of the most challenging aspects of the sport of agility is that the course is never laid out the same way twice. Even after Buck knows how to maneuver every agility obstacle, he won't know what order they will be in and will always have to take his cues from Carl. Handling is extremely important in this sport. Carl will have to think fast on his feet as he directs Buck, around the course at his best possible speed.

Agility has enormous spectator appeal and usually draws heavy applause and cheers, so Carl will also gain confidence in his ability to think and perform in front of an audience. Besides its benefits to Carl, agility is good for Buck, too. It trains and conditions him, making him happier, healthier, and more reliable.

In addition to its obvious rewards, Buck can earn titles for expertise in agility. Several organizations offer trials. The United States Dog Agility Association (USDAA) offers the titles Agility Dog (AD), Advanced Agility Dog (AAD), and Master Agility Dog (MAD).

To earn the AD, Buck, must complete one course within the time limit and without an error in the Starters or Novice Class. For the AAD, he must flawlessly complete three different and more difficult agility courses under two different judges within the assigned time limits. To earn the Master title, Carl and Buck will have to complete the most challenging courses seven times without making mistakes. (In agility, mistakes include errors such as knocking over a jump or taking a different obstacle than the one the handler indicated).

The National Club for Dog Agility (NCDA) competition, sanctioned by the United Kennel Club (UKC), also offers three agility titles. To earn the Agility I (AG-I) and Agility II (AG-II) titles, dogs must complete the course within the assigned time limit three different times and must earn a total of 170 points out of a possible perfect score of 200. The Agility II course has the greater degree of difficulty. Agility Trial Champion (ATCh) is the NCDA's highest

Katie Moureaux, 8, sends her Springer Spaniel, Alex, over a hurdle during agility competition. Katie trained Alex herself, and they have earned titles from several organizations. Juli Carralejo

title. It is earned by accumulating 100 points. Points are awarded for scores between 196 and 200. While only one point is offered for scores of 196, it isn't unusual to be presented with 10 points for a perfect 200.

If Buck is AKC registered, he is eligible for American Kennel Club agility titles. In order of difficulty they are Novice Agility Dog (NAD), Open Agility Dog (OAD), Agility Dog Excellent (ADX), and Master Agility Excellent (MAX). To earn the NAD, OAD, or ADX, Buck must obtain qualifying scores on three separate occasions under two different judges on a course of the designated difficulty. A qualifying score in AKC agility is 85 out of a possible 100 with no nonqualifying deductions. ADX dogs achieve the MAX by working with enough consistency to earn 10 more qualifying scores on the ADX course.

At trials run by all the agility organizations, dogs are awarded first through fourth place in each division in addition to earning qualifying scores for titles. That means agility trials can be noncompetitive, if Carl's sole aim is to have Buck qualify toward a title; or competitive, if Carl's goal is to win a placement. In fact, agility can be just as competitive as Carl desires and Buck can handle. For example, USDAA's Pedigree Grand Prix of Dog Agility holds regional events in major cities across the nation. Regional winners qualify for semifinals, and finalists compete at the prestigious Grand Prix.

PREPARATION AND PRACTICE

Because the sport requires so much large paraphernalia, such as jumps and tunnels, very few agility competitors own their own equipment. Consequently, Carl will have to join an agility club or take classes from a private instructor, in order to train on agility obstacles. But that's a good thing. Training alone, both Carl and Buck could adopt bad habits, and it's more difficult to retrain later than to begin correctly. Contact AKC, UKC, and USDAA (appendix I) to find out if there is an agility club in your area. Private teachers may be located through ads in the telephone book, the classifieds, pet-supply stores, or veterinarians' offices.

Becky Schroeder, 15, of Kalamazoo, Michigan, trains her Shetland Sheepdog, Saucey, on the A-frame. Saucey went on to earn her AG-1 title with a perfect score.

Earning even the first title offered by an agility organization entails a major commitment from you and Carl. Attending classes costs money, and agility trials require entry fees and travel. Carl will also need transportation to and from classes and practice sessions.

Carl's commitment will include time, patience, and the development of a positive attitude. Before attempting any obstacle work, he should teach Buck to respond to basic obedience commands such as come, sit, and down. It's best if these commands are taught and perfected in an area different from where agility training takes place, perhaps at an obedience class or at home.

Once Buck responds to basic commands, it may still take well over a year before he is ready for an agility trial. Patience and an upbeat attitude are essential. Good instructors set an example by being cheerful and motivational, and their programs incorporate many incentives such as toys, praise, and food to keep the dogs interested and happy.

EARNING TITLES

Before Carl enters his first agility trial he should know the rules, and he and Buck should be familiar with the obstacles. Although each organization has similar courses and obstacles, there are subtle differences in the layouts, the obstacles, and the rules. For rule books, a list of agility clubs sanctioned by each organization, and a calendar of upcoming agility events, send separate requests to USDAA, AKC, UKC, and NCDA (appendix I).

When Carl arrives at an event, he should study the layout of the obstacles for his division. Since the course will never repeat itself, he will have to plan a unique handling strategy at every trial, engineered to make the most of Buck's abilities. This will help them achieve the fastest possible time with the fewest mistakes. Well before his turn, Carl should give Buck a good exercise warm-up—enough to loosen his muscles but not enough to tire him.

Concentration combines with communication as Jamie Watters and Annie fly through a practice course.

When it's their turn, Carl and Buck will run the course alone and a judge will score them. Since many agility trials are held in conjunction with dog shows or other large events, Carl will have to keep his cool and follow his plan while performing for an enthusiastic audience. Buck may be somewhat less confident amid a cheering crowd, but if he senses that Carl is having fun and is pleased with him, he will probably respond to commands and signals as usual.

Sara Dege of Oakdale, Minnesota, and her Cavalier King Charles Spaniel, Trinket, competed in the USDAA Nationals in Houston, Texas, and did agility demonstrations for the Minnesota Timberwolves basketball team. Trinket also won a washer/dryer on the TV game show "That's My Dog."

If Carl is a little shaky, Buck will probably become nervous, too, and won't be able to give his best performance. Many kids are terrified at their first few trials, but eventually get over it. Conquering stage fright and learning to concentrate under pressure are two of the most subtle, yet enduring, rewards of agility participation.

LESSONS IN LIVING

"From working in agility, I've learned to be a fair winner and a good loser," says Marnie Kunz, 14, of St. Louis, Missouri. "I have been humbled and brought back to earth many times when I started to get overconfident and boastful. Spanky's mistakes on the agility course reflect my ability as a trainer, and whenever he seems perfectly trained, a new mistake pops up.

"I have learned that sometimes there are no shortcuts in life and things can only be achieved by long hours of hard work and repetition. In the end, hard work and determination really pay off.

"Also, Spanky has taught me to enjoy myself and not get carried away on earning titles and winning at trials. I started out thinking that winning first place was the only thing that

Marnie Kunz and her German Shepherd Dog, Spanky.

mattered, but when Spanky got a fourth place and still came out of the ring with a big grin and wagging tail, I realized he has fun just doing agility and being with me, whether he wins or not.

"To earn our Junior Handlers Elementary title with USDAA, Spanky and I must complete three rounds at three trials with no faults. So far, we haven't even completed one perfect round, but we won't give up!"

MORE THAN A CHAUFFEUR

Of course Marnie has to get to her events, and this is where her mother, Mrs. Chris Kunz, comes in. But does she mind?

"The role of chauffeur isn't fun," she says. "However, the time in the car with Marnie is an opportunity to discuss many things without sibling rivalry. It's a time to build self-esteem, to affirm, to laugh about trials and errors in general, as well as the dog agility events.

"Driving time allows a parent to encourage the child to be open to new friendship opportunities within the circle of people who share a common love of dogs and animals. The time and effort is worthwhile because agility training integrates physical and emotional development opportunities. Marnie has learned that trial and error is a way to acquire knowledge, make friends, and build self-confidence. She has also learned that successes and mistakes are both part of life. Keeping your balance, as well as the dog's, is a challenge and a reward."

Chapter 11

Tracking

Tracking combines training with instinct and results in a dog capable of using its incredible sense of smell to benefit humanity. While the Bloodhound is the breed of choice for professional tracking, all kinds of dogs are capable of succeeding in the sport, or in real-life emergencies. Gentle tracking dogs are sometimes needed to help search for lost persons, and many tracking clubs volunteer their services to agencies such as the local police or sheriff's department. Consequently, a variety of dogs, including toy breeds and mixed breeds, have saved lives by finding terrified toddlers and hopelessly lost hikers.

If Pepper is American Kennel Club registered and over six months old, she's eligible to earn AKC tracking titles through participation in noncompetitive tests. The American Mixed Breed Obedience Registry (AMBOR) offers similar tests and titles for mixed breed dogs. Passing an entry-level tracking test will earn Pepper a Tracking Dog title (TD), passing the advanced test will gain her a Tracking Dog Excellent (TDX), and passing a test on a variety of surfaces will earn her a Variable Surface Tracking title (VST). Each award includes a certificate from the registry, and the letters TD, TDX, or VST become an official suffix to her registered name.

TRAINING AND TRUSTING

Training a tracking dog is kind of like being a parent. When Tom ventures into the sport of tracking, he will begin by patiently teaching Pepper how to get on the right track and stay on it. Next, he will give her a bit more guidance and a lot of encouragement to keep her on the correct path. But later, after she knows how to stay on track, Tom will have to give Pepper her independence and trust her judgment.

Note: *Tracking demands a lot of patient training, a lot of time, and a good bit of space. For these and other reasons, there are not many children involved in the sport on a competitive level. However, so that you and your children know what's involved, here's a chapter on tracking. You can make up your own mind.*

Tom's role will be to teach Pepper to follow the path of a person who is minutes or hours ahead of her. To succeed, Tom will faithfully practice a program that encourages Pepper to find a certain scent and follow that scent (and only that scent) to its conclusion. Soon he will understand and rely on Pepper's body language to tell him if she's on the right track. Meanwhile, the better tracker Pepper becomes, the more oblivious she will be to anything but the track, and the less she will need Tom. In fact, the hardest part for Tom may be giving up all semblance of control and faithfully following Pepper. But he will have no choice. Realizing that humans simply cannot follow scent the way dogs can, good tracking handlers trust their dogs.

GOOD SCENTS

A dog's scenting ability is more than 15,000 times greater than a human's, and dogs are able to isolate each individual scent that makes up the whole. Tom may walk in the house and immediately realize that spaghetti sauce is cooking, but Pepper will decipher beef, tomatoes, onions, oregano, garlic, oil, salt, pepper, and more. That's why Customs agents work with dogs. The trained Customs dog sniffs a closed suitcase and smells not only the liberal dousing of perfume that was meant to confuse it, but the scent of the clothes inside, the body odors of the person who wore the clothes, the dry-cleaning chemicals, and every other scent that touched any item in that suitcase, including the drugs hidden inside the lining.

Have no fear. Tom and Pepper won't be called upon to search for hidden drug caches. But if they become an excellent team, and belong to a club that volunteers its services, they may be called upon to help find a lost person.

COMMITMENT AND EQUIPMENT

Tracking takes a moderate commitment in time and travel, and several inexpensive pieces of equipment. Tom will need transportation to classes, practice sessions, and tests. Equipment includes a couple of long, thin dowels with a strip of colored cloth or plastic attached to the top (used as flags to mark the beginning and end of the track); a six-foot lead (for the first few days of training); a 20- to 40-foot lead (for training and for testing); a nonrestrictive tracking harness (available through pet-supply companies); an open, uncrowded place to practice, such as a park, field, or large yard; a patient person to serve as tracklayer; several articles, such as a soft hat, gloves, and wallet, for Pepper to find; and a pocketful of training treats per practice.

It's best if training sessions follow a prescribed routine fashioned by a tracking instructor. Good programs start with an easy track of 10 yards for large dogs and about half that for small dogs and puppies. The dogs are never rushed, and the distance gradually increases following each successful session.

It's not unusual for a routine to entail five or six brief training sessions a week until Pepper obviously understands her role. After that, two or three practices weekly will do nicely. Too much practice may bore Pepper and dampen her enthusiasm for the sport. Conditioning is also vital for tracking dogs and their handlers, so on the days when Tom and Pepper don't practice, they should enjoy a long walk.

TRACKING TESTS

If Tom and Pepper want to try for AKC tracking titles, they will need transportation to a minimum of two tracking events. Dogs must pass one certification evaluation given by an AKC tracking judge before they are eligible to enter a test, but they only have to pass the actual test one time to earn the TD title. At the test, articles are dropped on the track by the tracklayer and dogs track one at a time. The length of the TD test track is between 440 and 500 yards with three to five turns, and the scent will be between 30 minutes and two hours old.

Pepper will perform wearing a tracking harness and lead, and Tom will walk between 20 and 40 feet behind her, holding the lead. Tom may give Pepper low-key verbal commands and verbal encouragement but may not do anything to indicate the location or direction of the track. Two judges will evaluate Pepper simultaneously. She will succeed if she follows the scent left by the tracklayer and finds the article (a glove or wallet) at the end of the track. The requirements for the TDX title include a longer, older track with more turns.

TIPS FOR TRACKING

Tom should prepare for any eventuality because tracking is an outdoor sport held under a variety of weather conditions. When attending tests, he should wear comfortable clothing and carry an extra jacket or sweater, a slicker, and well-broken-in all-weather boots in case the weather changes. It's also a good idea to bring something simple to eat and drink.

Pepper will need her tracking equipment, water from home, and a dish. It's smart to carry a portion-packed plastic bag of her regular food in case of emergency, even if you plan to be home before feeding time. Tom should exercise Pepper lightly before the test, then keep her comfortably in the shade until her turn.

GETTING ON TRACK

To find a club where Tom can learn how to train Pepper for tracking, contact the American Kennel Club (appendix 1) and request a copy of their tracking regulations booklet and a geographical list of tracking clubs (many are combined with obedience clubs). Use the list to find the clubs that offer tracking classes or practices closest to you.

If Pepper will be tracking through the American Mixed Breed Obedience Registry (appendix 1), request an information packet and the location of the AMBOR club nearest you.

Teaching Pepper to track is a sport, and earning titles is a challenge, but using the finished product to help find lost persons could be the beginning of an adventure.

Chapter 12

Puppy Raiser for a Service or Guide Dog Organization

N umerous nonprofit organizations across the country breed and train guide dogs to lead the blind, hearing dogs for the deaf, and service dogs to help the disabled. Some of these groups rely on volunteers, called puppy raisers, to give their puppies a good start. Their task is to take on a foster puppy and raise it until it is a confident and mannerly adult dog, capable of learning and performing complex tasks.

Canine Companions for Independence (CCI), for example, trains dogs to serve people who have disabilities other than blindness, and provides three types of assistance dogs: service, hearing, and social.

Service dogs perform practical tasks for people with physical disabilities. Their work entails opening doors, picking up objects, carrying a purse or wallet, operating light switches, and many other jobs especially suited to their owners' needs.

Hearing dogs wake up their deaf masters when the alarm clock goes off, and let them know when someone is at the door or when the telephone rings.

Social dogs help autistic or learning-impaired masters relate to other people. In addition to their specialized training, all three types of dogs provide vital companionship.

CCI puppy Eisner (right) with his two trainers. Becky Schroeder socializes him and teaches him basic commands. Saucey (front) helps him learn house manners.

The assistance dogs used by Canine Companions for Independence are carefully bred by the organization and then raised in private homes. Puppy raisers, many of whom are children and teenagers, are a cornerstone of the program. Their work is crucial, because the first several months of a dog's life significantly affect its attitude and temperament at maturity.

To grow up loving, happy, healthy, and confident, puppies need a lot of affection and attention, so puppy raisers socialize their dogs by taking them along almost everywhere they go. The puppies always wear their yellow CCI cape when outside the home, and sometimes this gains them admittance to a facility where dogs would otherwise be off-limits. In fact, some schools even allow students to bring their CCI puppies to class with them.

Puppy raisers also attend basic training classes created especially for them. There they learn training skills so they can teach the pups house manners and obedience to simple commands. At the same time, the puppies learn to get along with strangers and other dogs. Play exercises (games that increase a puppy's ability to work later in life) are part of the fun for the young trainers and the puppies.

Since the bond each puppy develops with its puppy raiser is vital to its future success as an assistance dog, CCI stipulates that the puppy must live indoors and sleep in the puppy raiser's bedroom. This creates a strong bond between the puppy and its human partner, laying the groundwork for the close working relationship it will develop with its disabled owner.

Becky Schroeder talks about that special bond: "The first Canine Companion for Independence that I raised and trained was Imke, a 10-week-old male Golden Retriever who instantly won my heart. He began obedience training with my 4-H club and with the

Becky Schroeder attends a 4-H meeting with Imke, her foster puppy from Canine Companions for Independence.

Kalamazoo Dog Training Club. My dog, Saucey, helped with Imke's house manners, as she was in charge. Imke went with us everywhere, and when people asked why he was allowed in a restaurant or store, I was happy to tell them about service dogs and the CCI program. I also took him to agility classes to help build his self-confidence, and he accompanied us on visits to the nursing home.

"One of the hardest things I had to do was return Imke to the CCI Training Center in Delaware, Ohio. I checked on him frequently and always got a wonderful progress report. Out of thirteen dogs turned in that March, Imke was one of seven that graduated, and he is currently living and working in Cape Coral, Florida. I was even asked to be a guest speaker at his graduation! We got the opportunity to meet Imke's new family and had dinner with them after graduation. We still keep in touch and I feel really good about it all. Now I have a second CCI dog, a yellow Lab named Eisner."

THE CCI SCHEDULE

Volunteer puppy raisers receive their foster puppies when the pups are eight weeks old, and the volunteers love, socialize, and train the puppies for the next 15 to 18 months. Then the young dogs return to CCI for complete physical examinations and six months of advanced training. From then on, the puppy raisers don't see the dogs again until graduation day.

During advanced training at CCI, the dog learns numerous skills, and its personality and special abilities are noted by the staff. Finally, a group of disabled recipients attend a three-week training course where they learn how to work with a dog. Each student works with a variety of dogs for the first few days, while the CCI instructors evaluate the teamwork between the students and each dog. Then each student is matched with the dog best suited to his or her personality and needs, and days of intensive practice follow.

After a student learns how to give and enforce commands that the dog already knows, the team practices in public places such as malls and city streets. The students also learn special techniques so they can expand their dog's range of commands to meet their unique needs. Finally, before graduating and taking the Canine Companion home, each student must demonstrate the ability to take good care of his or her dog.

GRADUATING TO INDEPENDENCE

On graduation day, puppy raisers witness the results of their loving efforts. First they meet the dog's new master, seeing firsthand how

Heather Hennes, 1994 National 4-H Guide Dog Raising/Training Scholarship winner, with her "change of career" guide dog puppy, Lucas. When Lucas didn't make it through the guide dog program, Heather took him back as her own dog. Now they are preparing for AKC obedience competition. Heather has been in the 4-H Guide Dog project for seven years and has raised five puppies for Guide Dogs for the Blind of San Rafael, California.

"My mom told me that the feelings we get at a guide dog graduation are sort of like a mother feels when one of her kids has done something great," says Heather Hennes, a 17-year-old from Santa Rosa, California. "I am really proud of my puppy, yet at the same time, I feel sad, because the pup is going on to another phase of its life. My mom says it's a lot like the way you feel when your son or daughter graduates from high school or college!"

Heather's mother, Sandra, adds, "Don't get involved with puppy raising if your child is the type to lose interest or not follow through. Before a child gets as involved as Heather has, the parent should be aware of not letting them do it just to teach them responsibility. Otherwise parents end up doing all the work for their child and the child doesn't benefit.

"There have been many difficult times. It was really tough when Heather was 11 and the guide dog puppy she was raising had to be put to sleep because of severe hip dysplasia. There have also been chewed shoes, normal puppy messes, and various expenses.

"But the pluses have been great! It's wonderful to watch the bonding between Heather and the puppies. I feel she's learned so much more from these experiences than children not involved with dogs ever learn."

the partnership enables the person to overcome physical and social barriers. Realizing their work helped this person attain a new, independent life is an emotionally rewarding experience few kids ever forget.

During graduation ceremonies, puppy raisers officially present the dogs they raised to their new partners. Then, through tears of happiness, some immediately sign up to raise another Canine Companion. Beware, it can become addictive. There are cases where parents still raise assistance puppies even though their kids grew up and moved out years ago.

A FAMILY AFFAIR

While it may be Mike's desire to raise a future guide or service dog, and everyone has agreed that the bulk of the responsibility will be his, family support is absolutely essential. The commitment generally lasts between 14 and 18 months, and you will pay for veterinary and feeding expenses while fostering the puppy and comply with the organization's nutritional guidelines. Mike will need transportation to take the puppy to the required training classes as well as out into the world for socialization (getting it accustomed to different people, other dogs, and all types of sights and sounds, including stairs, elevators, malls, and downtown shopping districts). But that's just a small part of the support Mike may need.

Robin Rosebrock, a 13-year-old from Mariposa, California, talks about her experience. "Friar, a male Golden Retriever, lived with us for 15 months of socialization and training. He is now back at Guide Dogs for the Blind, finishing his training. The day I returned him I was filled with conflicting emotions. I was happy that I had been able to do something for someone else and proud of the job I'd done. But although I wanted Friar to be accepted, a part of me wanted him to fail so I could keep him. I was sad when we parted, but they put Pepita, a female Labrador Retriever puppy, into my arms, and she licked away my tears. This will be another learning and loving experience for the next 13 to 16 months."

Raising a puppy can be frustrating at times and fabulous at times, and Mike may need emotional support to help him through all of those times. He'll need encouragement when the puppy "goofs" after everyone thought it was housebroken, or forgets commands in class after performing perfectly at home. He'll need understanding when the puppy showers him with affection and he gives back the same, knowing full well that one day this wonderful puppy will grow up and have to leave.

Robin Rosebrock and 18-month-old Friar on the day he returned to Guide Dogs for the Blind.

Sometimes there are major disappointments. For example, Mike may have cared for, socialized, and trained his foster puppy well, but the puppy may still not become a guide or service dog. After puppies leave their foster homes they undergo complete physical examinations and are removed from the program if they are defective in any way. Also, some physically perfect puppies don't make it through the mental rigors of advanced training. While the guide and service dog organizations always prepare their puppy raisers for these possibilities, nothing takes the place of supportive parents if sad news arrives. Simply reminding Mike that he did all he could and you are proud of his efforts could help the healing begin.

When a dog is deemed unfit for a service career, most organizations give the puppy raiser's family first refusal on adoption. To avoid making a hasty decision on an emotional issue, discuss this possibility in advance and decide whether or not your family would want the dog permanently. Service organizations usually have a waiting list of adoptive homes, so there is no need to take yourself on a guilt trip if you don't want the dog.

A BIG, *BRIEF* COMMITMENT

While raising a future guide or service dog is a major commitment, it's all over in less than 18 months. If Mike wants a dog but you've been saying no because he'll leave for college in a few years and you'll be stuck dog-sitting, consider this: Becoming a foster family for a

Fifteen-year-old Mandy Gonzalez of Upper Marlboro, Maryland, wrote, "The dogs we have raised and trained for the Guide Dog Foundation are Em, Reelie, Hadley, Tarnell, and Doodles. We received a letter and picture from Carol, the blind woman who got our first puppy, Em. We were all so excited to learn of our great success with our first guide dog. Then, when we got word about Reelie, it was the greatest news in the whole wide world. Reelie was so good she had been pulled out of the program to be used for breeding more puppies for the Guide Dog Foundation. We were overcome with joy! But we were all sad when it was time for the 'Had Man' to go. Hadley was a great little dog."

Thea Gonzalez, 16, and her sisters Mandy and Sarah, are raising their fifth puppy for the Guide Dog Foundation of Smithtown, New York.

Sarah Gonzalez socializes the family's first puppy-raising project, a Lab named Em.

service dog organization gives Mike a temporary dog and expert guidance on how to raise and train one. Mike gets his dog experience, and the dog leaves before he goes to college. Whether or not the dog graduates, Mike will have accepted the challenge of taking it from an unruly youngster to a cooperative adult, and the experience will give him confidence, patience, and an increased sense of responsibility.

GETTING STARTED

A list of several service dog organizations that may need volunteers to raise their puppies appears in appendix 1. Write or call them to find out their requirements. Though most of them accept children as puppy raising volunteers, parental consent is necessary if the child is under 18, and the parents are ultimately responsible for the puppy's welfare.

Chapter 13

Junior Showmanship

Junior showmanship is the only competitive canine event created exclusively for kids. It was introduced in 1932 so dog show exhibitors' children would have something to do while their parents groomed and showed dogs. Today, junior showmanship is offered at most dog shows and has become a highly competitive, demanding, and rewarding pursuit. Since many shows draw entries of well over a thousand dogs, the myriad breeds and the multitude of handlers and spectators are all part of the day's excitement for the young handlers.

As a junior handler, Judy will be judged on her ability to handle Max in the show ring. This includes presenting Max to the judge in the same way that he would be properly handled in the breed ring, and making him look his best both stacked (posed) and moving (trotting). To perform well, Judy will have to follow the judge's directions. This entails knowing basic ring routines and gaiting patterns and making intelligent use of the available space.

Members of the Working Paws 4-H Club of Saranac, Michigan, practicing for showmanship competition.

It won't take Judy long to realize that being prepared, confident, and businesslike also count toward a winning performance. You may hardly recognize your neatly dressed, combed, and polished teenager when she enters the ring to vie with the competition.

Competing in junior showmanship provides many kids with long-term rewards. Those who aspire to handle show dogs improve their skills in the show ring and learn how to properly groom and handle their own breed. Other skills are universal, so children who eventually leave dog events also benefit from their junior showmanship experiences. For example, the ability to maintain poise and think clearly while performing under pressure could be a career booster, and practicing good sportsmanship, whether winning or losing, is vital to making and keeping friends.

COMPETITIVE CLASSES

Junior showmanship classes are offered at AKC, UKC, and mixed-breed registry dog shows, and prizes (usually ribbons) are awarded for first through fourth place. To be eligible for competition at AKC events, Judy must be at least 10 years old and younger than 18. In addition, Max must be an AKC-registered dog, owned by Judy or a close relative, and eligible to compete in dog shows or obedience trials. Female dogs in season may not compete.

AKC's Novice Junior Showmanship class is for exhibitors who have not won three first-place awards in competition in a Novice Class. The Open Class is for those who already have won three first-place awards in Novice. When junior showmanship classes are further divided by age, the Novice and Open Junior classes are for kids from 10 to under 14 years of age, and the Novice and Open Senior classes go from 14 to under 18 years old. Classes offered by the mixed-breed registries are similar to AKC's but do not require a purebred dog.

UKC Junior Showmanship rules allow children as young as two years old to participate, but stipulate that handlers must maintain control of their dogs. Parents may accompany children under eight years old into the show ring, and in the youngest divisions all the children receive a ribbon for participating.

Competitive UKC classes include the junior division for children from 8 to 12 years old, and the senior division for teenagers from 13 to 17. Although junior showmanship dogs do not have to be family owned, UKC recommends that Max be owned by Judy or a member of her immediate family.

When a Best Junior Handler award is offered at any show, the first-place winners in each division compete against each other for the prize.

Robin Rosebrock, 13, of Mariposa, California, says she was born to "go to the dogs." Her dad is a veterinarian and her mom is an animal health technician who also breeds and shows Irish Wolfhounds and teaches training classes. Robin learned to walk holding on to one of the family wolfhounds and used to nap in a cradle amid the dog and cat noises at her parents' veterinary hospital.

"But even though there were always lots of dogs around, my folks made me wait until I was older and showed them that I would be responsible before I got my own dog," Robin says.

Robin got Honey, a Whippet, for her ninth birthday and used her in a 4-H Dog Care and Training Project. They also learned junior showmanship and had fun at matches. When Robin was 10, they started competing at AKC shows and quickly advanced from the Novice Junior to the Open Junior Class. Today, Honey is also a successful lure courser.

Robin Rosebrock and her Whippet, Honey, pose for a victory picture following a first-place win in AKC Junior Showmanship.

PREPARING TO COMPETE

Becoming highly competitive in junior showmanship demands a major commitment, while participating only in nearby shows (possible in large urban areas where there are frequent shows within a 50-mile radius) entails a moderate commitment. Before competing,

Judy should visit a few dog shows. There she should watch the juniors being judged and also study the judging of Max's breed and group, with special emphasis on how the handlers accentuate their dog's best qualities.

Judy should also study the standard for Max's breed, because knowing his best and worst features (his attributes and his faults) will help her emphasize the good and minimize the bad—an important part of good handling. Breed standards present a word picture of what the ideal dog of each breed looks like, and any variation from perfection is considered a fault. Since no dog is perfect, one mark of an excellent handler is knowing the dog well enough to make its strong points stand out and its faults fade into the background. If Max is an AKC breed, his standard is in *The Complete Dog Book* (appendix 2), available in almost every library. If he is UKC registered, his standard should be available through his UKC breed club. Contact the United Kennel Club (appendix 1) to locate the UKC club specializing in Max's breed.

Handling classes are practically a necessity for aspiring juniors, and the best way to find them is through your local all-breed club. Contact AKC, UKC, or AMBOR (appendix 1), depending on how Max is registered, and request a list of dog clubs in your area. Even if your local club doesn't offer special classes just for juniors, it may offer conformation classes for people preparing their dogs for the breed ring. Such classes will do just fine, and if Judy asks, the instructor may even help her interpret Max's breed standard. In addition to classes, there are many books available on junior showmanship. They make an excellent addition to Judy's education but will not take the place of attending class.

Before competing in AKC Junior Showmanship, Judy will need a junior-handler number. This is obtained by calling AKC's Events Records Department at (212) 696-8281, 282, or 283. Judy should request a Junior Showmanship rule book at the same time and study it thoroughly before entering an event.

Some dog clubs hold matches where junior showmanship is offered. Matches are similar to dog shows but are less formal and not so crowded. Also, since no points toward conformation championships are awarded, there is less tension in the air. Consequently, matches are a great place to practice handling skills before trying them out at a real dog show.

ENTERING A SHOW

To find AKC dog shows offering junior showmanship, Judy should send a postcard to each of the show superintendents listed in appendix 1, asking to be placed on their mailing lists. Soon premium lists containing entry forms will fill your mailbox. Also, *The AKC Gazette* (appendix 2), a monthly magazine published by the American Kennel Club, includes an events calendar for the coming months.

UKC shows with competition for juniors are advertised in UKC's bimonthly magazine, *Bloodlines* (appendix 2), which includes lists of upcoming shows.

If Max is a mixed breed, contact the American Mixed Breed Obedience Registry (AMBOR) and/or the Mixed Breed Dog Club of California (appendix 2) and request a list of coming events. They will also tell you how to register Max so he can be shown.

IN THE RING

Junior showmanship looks much like the regular classes of a dog show with one major exception. In the regular classes, only the dog is judged, while in junior showmanship only Judy will be judged, and Max's quality (or lack of it) should not matter one bit. Even so, he should be groomed as if he were a show dog about to compete in the breed ring. While the judge will not evaluate Judy's grooming and trimming skills, Max should look as handsome as she can make him.

During competition, Judy will be asked to demonstrate her handling ability in three areas. First, she will move (gait) Max around the ring with the rest of the class. Then, when it's her turn, she will present him in a standing position for the judge's examination and move him individually in the pattern(s) requested by the judge. Judy must firmly but gently control Max at all times, be courteous to the judge and the other handlers, and be alert to Max's handling needs and the judge's commands. She will be judged on her ability to make Max look his best both standing (stacked) and gaiting. Top handlers make their dogs stand out, not themselves.

If Judy becomes a winning handler with the ambition to make it to the pinnacle of her sport, AKC Junior Showmanship can become a consuming avocation. The magic of Westminster, a prestigious dog show held every February at Madison Square Garden in New York City, is what keeps many kids practicing and showing. It takes eight first-place wins at AKC shows during the previous year to qualify for competition at Westminster, and winning those eight shows keeps many juniors focused on improving their skills. It also costs money in entry fees and traveling. This sport can be tough on parents. But it's sure hard to fault Judy for aspiring to handle Max at Madison Square Garden provided that it's her idea, and she willingly devotes the time and effort necessary to qualify for the honor.

Chapter 14

Dog Showing

At shows, dogs are judged on their conformation (overall appearance and structure). Every breed of dog has its own standard of excellence. Think of it as a word picture, or blueprint, of what constitutes a perfect specimen. The national breed club that represents each breed drafts the standard, and the judges simply act as interpreters. They compare each competing dog to their visualization of the ideal specimen of the breed, as detailed by its breed standard. The winner is the dog that, in the judge's opinion, comes closest to the faultless animal the standard describes.

Dog show judging is entirely subjective, as dogs win or lose on the basis of how they are perceived by a particular judge. Sometimes it's hard for kids who grow up playing basketball or softball (where everyone knows and understands the score), to get used to subjective judging.

While dog shows are beautiful—even inspiring—to those who understand them, they can seem crowded and confusing to the uninitiated. Think of them as elimination contests, and they will make

Kerrin Winter stacks Teasel, her German Wirehaired Pointer, during competition at an AKC show several years ago. Since this photo was taken, Kerrin turned her love of animals into a profession as a photographer.

sense. During the first part of a dog show, each breed of dog is judged individually at its assigned time in its assigned ring. Since there are so many breeds of dogs, judging occurs in several rings simultaneously. Even so, finding the breeds you want to see is easy. Just buy a show catalog when you arrive and turn to the judging program. It lists every breed entered in the show and tells you where and when (ring and time) each will be exhibited. Watching your favorite breeds compete is as easy as arriving at the right ring at the appointed time, and anyone planning to exhibit should attend a show or two first to learn the procedure.

UNDERSTANDING A DOG SHOW

At AKC shows, six different regular classes are offered for male and female dogs in each breed. Males are exhibited before females. Classes, in order of appearance, are:

Puppy (six- to nine-month-old or nine- to twelve-month-old dogs)

Twelve to Eighteen Months

Novice (never won a blue ribbon in any of the other classes, or has won less than three ribbons in the Novice Class)

Bred by Exhibitor (the exhibitor is also the breeder)

American-Bred (dog's parents bred in America and the dog was born in America)

Open (any dog of that breed)

First through fourth place is awarded in each of these classes.

After all regular classes of the breed have been judged, the first-place winners of each class compete against each other to determine which one is best of the winning males and the winning females. Championship points are awarded to the *Winners Dog* and the *Winners Bitch* (the top male and the top female in the regular classes).

Finally, the two winners return to the ring for the "Specials" Class. Now they compete against each other and against dogs that are already champions for the breed's highest honor—Best of Breed. Three awards are usually presented at the end of breed competition. *Best of Breed* is the dog judged best of all the entered dogs of that breed. *Best of Winners* is the dog judged best between the Winners Dog and Winners Bitch, and *Best of Opposite Sex* is the best dog that is the opposite sex from the Best of Breed winner. Only the top-winning dog, the Best of Breed, advances to compete in Group competition.

At AKC shows, the breeds are divided into seven Groups: Sporting, Hound, Working, Terrier, Toy, Non-sporting, and Herding. Following breed judging, the Best of Breed winners compete against each other by Group until only seven dogs are left in competition—the seven Group winners. These seven superior dogs then compete against each other for *Best in Show*.

Thus, even though a dog show opens in the morning with an entry of over 2,000 dogs, by sundown only one remains undefeated—the dog deemed Best in Show. But there are many other winners. For example, dogs and bitches (proper terminology for males and females) of many breeds will have won championship points.

The majority of dogs showing in conformation are competing for points toward their championship. When a dog wins enough points to earn that honor, it is awarded a championship certificate. From then on, the dog is officially recorded as a Champion of Record, and the title Ch. (Champion) becomes a prefix of its official name. At AKC shows, it takes 15 points, including two majors (wins of three to five points) under at least three different judges to earn the treasured title. The amount of points a dog wins at one show depends upon how many dogs of its own breed it defeats that day, and no more than five points are ever won at a single show.

RING PROCEDURE

When showing King to the judges, Jean will hold the show lead (a style of leash used to exhibit dogs) in her left hand and wear an arm band with King's number on her left upper arm. A steward (judge's helper) will call King's class into the ring and may ask the handlers to line up in the same order as they appear in the show catalog. Ring procedure varies somewhat depending on the judge, but generally the handlers stack (pose) the dogs as soon as they enter the ring. On the judge's command, all the dogs are gaited (trotted at their most attractive speed) around the ring together, one behind the other.

Following group gaiting, the judge usually begins the individual examinations. Jean will prepare King for examination by stacking him in his most attractive stance, taking into consideration his breed and his individual attributes. During the examination, the judge will check King's bite and feel his bone structure and musculature. Because King is a male dog, the judge will also check his testicles. Males must have two descended testicles to compete in the breed ring.

After the examination, the judge will ask Jean to gait King in a particular pattern. The pattern (usually a triangle, an L shape, or down-and-back) will be the same for every dog, so it's a good idea for handlers to arrive early and watch their judge's ring procedure. If that isn't possible, and Jean doesn't understand the judge's request, all she has to do is ask the judge to repeat it.

Eleven-year-old Lia Temarantz says her favorite sports are skiing and dog exhibiting. Here she handles Tootsie, her Lhasa Apso, at an AKC show. Courtesy of Temarantz Studio.

After each dog has been gaited individually, and all the dogs are stacked again, the judge may render a decision by announcing the first- through fourth-place winners, or may have a few dogs gait again before selecting the winners. Jean should remain near the ring if King wins a blue ribbon because he will be called back to compete in the Winners Class.

LEARNING HOW TO SHOW

No dog fully epitomizes its breed standard, and the handler's job is to emphasize the dog's strong points while playing down its faults. To present King well, Jean will have to know where he lives up to his breed standard and where he is lacking (his individual virtues and faults). She will also have to learn coat conditioning and grooming procedures for King's breed, or have a professional show (not pet) groomer prepare him for competition. To allow himself to be presented well, King will have to be trained in ring procedure, then conditioned to keep his cool while performing amid strange dogs and crowds of people.

Books and articles about handling at dog shows are extremely helpful, but they won't take the place of class instruction. Handlers who always work alone often practice minor errors without realizing

Ami Patricia Temarantz, 7, handles Rachel, CD, TD, CGC, a Toy Poodle, in the Parade of Title Holders at a Poodle specialty show. Courtesy of Temarantz Studio.

they are making them, while instructors are able to point out these mistakes. A good conformation instructor will know the traditional method of handling King's breed and will help Jean understand and interpret the standard. A good teacher will also show Jean how to enhance King's attributes and showmanship, minimize his faults, and find his most attractive gaiting speed. Meanwhile, attending classes will teach King to remain steady in the company of other dogs while different people examine him.

Many all-breed dog clubs offer conformation instruction and practice sessions. To find a class near you, write to the American Kennel Club (appendix 1) and request a geographical list of AKC show and obedience clubs and a copy of "Rules Applying to Dog Shows." To use the geographical list, look up the clubs in your state and contact those nearest you about classes or meetings. Conformation classes may also be advertised in the classified section of the newspaper, or by flyer in veterinarians' waiting rooms or pet-supply stores. Before entering a show, read the sections of the rule book that apply to exhibiting dogs, especially the conditions that affect the eligibility of dogs.

Upcoming AKC dog shows are listed in the "Events Calendar," a supplement of the monthly publication *The AKC Gazette* (appendix 2). To receive premium lists and entry blanks for AKC dog shows, Jean should send a postcard to each of the show superintendents (appendix 1) and ask to be put on their mailing lists.

UNITED KENNEL CLUB (UKC) SHOWS

Although class divisions and point schedules for championships differ, judging procedure is similar to that of AKC shows. Write to the United Kennel Club (UKC) for a rule book. *Bloodlines*, UKC's bimonthly publication (appendix 2), advertises upcoming shows.

SHOW QUALITY

The purpose of dog shows is to preserve the best qualities of the breeds and possibly even improve them. So, no matter how well Jean handles, King will have to be an exceptionally fine example of his breed if he is to become a champion.

Most dogs destined for the show ring are bred by dedicated breeders and sold as show quality. If King was not purchased with dog showing in mind, he has a mighty slim chance of winning the points he needs to become a conformation champion, no matter how pretty or well groomed he is. Of course there have been exceptions. If you believe King may be show quality, take him to a conformation class and ask the instructor and the other breeders for their honest opinions. If the opinions are mixed, contact a professional handler who has a good reputation among people who own your breed. Even if a professional critique costs money, it will be much less expensive, and certainly less frustrating, than traveling to show after show without a chance of success.

JUNIOR SHOWMANSHIP

If Jean has her heart set on showing, and you have no intention of adding a show dog to your family, there is a solution. Jean can have the entire dog show experience by entering junior showmanship (a complete discussion of this activity is in chapter 13). In the showmanship ring, she and King will perform exactly as if they were in the breed ring, but Jean's handling ability will be judged, not King's conformation. Handling in either the breed ring or the showmanship ring will help Jean learn to think under pressure, perform for an audience, and practice good sportsmanship.

Even if King is a super specimen of his breed, winning a championship isn't easy, and it costs money in entry fees and traveling expenses. In fact, with some breeds (those exhibited almost exclusively by professional handlers), it may be an impossible dream for a young, novice handler with her first show dog. Nevertheless, if King is show quality and well prepared for the ring, and Jean handles smoothly, they might win some ribbons in their class.

Besides showing her own dog, a Whippet, in junior showmanship and lure coursing, 13-year-old Robin Rosebrock helps her mom show their Irish Wolfhounds. In this victory photo, Mom is handling the Best of Breed winner and Robin is handling Best of Winners and Opposite Sex.

But dog showing offers more important rewards than ribbons, trophies, and championship titles. In addition to helping Jean become poised in public, exhibiting in conformation will make her aware of scientific fields such as gen-etics and heredity. Chances are she will learn how to read and interpret pedigrees, and her powers of observation will be enhanced as she studies King's fine points and compares him to the competition.

Chapter 15

Hunting Tests

Humans and dogs have hunted together since before recorded history. In fact, one of the first records of their partnership are drawings found on the walls of caves. Through hundreds of years of selective breeding, three specific types of hunting dogs emerged. Today each type is cherished for its own abilities, purpose, and style.

If Bo is a registered dog of one of the traditional hunting breeds, he is eligible to participate in noncompetitive hunting tests. At these tests, dogs are judged on how closely they meet an acceptable standard of performance. In order to evaluate Bo's ability to be a fine hunting companion, the tests will assess his natural hunting instinct as well as his training.

Retrievers, spaniels, and pointing dogs each take a different form of hunting test, with features designed to cultivate their specific abilities. Most of the handlers at these tests are not hunters, but people who enjoy outdoor sports and believe the hunting breeds should still be able to do the work they were originally bred to perform.

Michael (Mikie) Moroz, 5, handles Gumbo, a Labrador Retriever, at a Young Hunter test.

The test setting is always as close to natural hunting conditions as possible, so the dogs can showcase their inborn talents. A sporting dog's natural quarry is game birds, and farm-raised game birds are used at hunting tests and shot for the dogs by qualified, designated gunners. It's important that Sunny be aware of this before deciding if hunting tests are the right sport for her. She should also understand why preserving the abilities of hunting dogs is so important. A good dog is vital to game-bird conservation because it ensures that wherever a shot bird falls—in thick brush, tall grass, or water—it will be found and retrieved, never wasted. Thus a hunter with a bag limit of three will have to shoot only three to get three.

HUNTING TEST TITLES

The first hunting test title offered by the American Kennel Club is Junior Hunter (JH). Dogs of any age are welcome to enter this test, as the word *Junior* refers to experience and training, not age. To merit the JH, Bo must earn qualifying scores at four AKC-approved Junior Hunting tests. Each time Bo qualifies, he will receive a qualifying ribbon in blaze (hunter) orange. Upon completion of the requirements, AKC will issue a certificate proclaiming Bo a Junior Hunter. From then on, the letters JH will be a suffix to his name, and he will officially be known as Bo, JH.

A grinning John Henry Lovelace III (Trae), 4, of Waco, Texas, displays the blaze orange qualifying ribbon earned by Maggie, the family Labrador Retriever. Trae loves to throw the field dummies (practice objects for dogs to retrieve) for Maggie, his mom and dad's dog, and Max, his own five-month-old puppy.

Earning the Junior Hunter title will take a moderate to heavy commitment. Much depends on how much basic training Bo already has, how strong a hunting instinct he harbors, and how easily Sunny learns the fundamentals of training and handling him in the field. The sport involves driving to practice sessions, traveling to tests, and paying entry fees, in addition to class or club fees, for practice sessions. But the rewards are greater than just orange qualifying ribbons and a title. Participating in hunting tests will give Sunny a healthy, outdoor hobby where she meets true sportspeople of all ages. It also gives Bo a chance to prove he can do the job he was originally created for.

If Sunny counts the days to the next test, and Bo squirms with anticipation en route to his field sessions, they don't have to stop when they earn the Junior Hunter title. Hunting tests have three progressive levels, and each level provides a significantly greater challenge. A successful Junior Hunter can advance to Senior Hunter, and finally to the highly prized Master Hunter title.

The following sections will summarize how retrievers, pointing breeds, and spaniels are evaluated at the AKC Junior Hunter level. In addition to AKC hunting tests, other organizations offer noncompetitive tests for the sporting breeds and some of them are listed later in this chapter. While each organization uses its own tests and scoring system, they all have similarities since they evaluate the basic attributes hunting dogs should show in the field.

EVALUATING RETRIEVERS

A retriever's traditional work is retrieving any type of game bird brought down by the hunter under all kinds of conditions. If Bo is registered as one of the following breeds, he is eligible for entry in retriever hunting tests: Chesapeake Bay Retriever, Curly-Coated Retriever, Flat-Coated Retriever, Golden Retriever, Labrador Retriever, and Irish Water Spaniel.

In the Junior Hunting test, Bo will be required to perform four single marks (retrieves). Two of them will be on land and two on water. Tests in the junior category simulate real but rather elementary hunting situations, and retrieves are usually 100 yards or less. Senior and Master tests simulate progressively more difficult hunting situations.

TAKING THE TEST (RETRIEVERS)

Retrievers are evaluated in four categories at hunting tests. The first is called marking, or memory. To earn a passing score in this category, Bo will have to demonstrate that he remembers where the bird fell by going directly to the area.

"As a mother and veterinarian, I'm glad to see my son Mikie work with animals, as I believe that caring for a pet encourages children to become responsible and develop tenderness for others," says Sharon Moroz, DVM, of Hampton, Georgia. "My husband and I have taken him to hunting tests since he was three months old. Now some of the retriever club members tell newcomers that they can get advice from Mikie on dog training, as they have watched him grow and learn how to handle dogs. We feel that encouraging him to work the dogs with us gives the family a hobby we can all enjoy together.

"Mikie is also learning that there is work involved in keeping dogs as he has to help feed them and clean kennels. While not his best activity, he knows he is expected to help with these chores."

Gumbo retrieves a bird for 6-year-old Mikie Moroz during a Young Hunter test.

The second category on the evaluation form is style. Bo is stylish if he is alert, eager to work, enters the water without hesitation, retrieves speedily, and obviously enjoys his job.

Perseverance, courage, and hunting combine to make up the third category. Bo has these attributes if he is willing to work areas of rough cover (thick or prickly vegetation), doesn't mind entering cold water, and continues to do his job (find and retrieve the bird) without losing interest or slowing down.

The fourth and final category is trainability, with subheads of steadiness, control, response, and delivery. In this category, Bo is scored on the abilities he learned through training (his acquired rather than instinctive attributes).

Bo should demonstrate that he is under Sunny's control by being obedient and having good manners on the line, and by responding to Sunny's directional signals. He must also be unafraid of the sound of gunfire.

When Bo is on the line (waiting beside Sunny for a bird to be downed by the gunners), he should remain steady. It's great if he shows eagerness and excitement, but he must still stay in place until Sunny gives him the signal to retrieve. She may keep her hand on his collar but should not have to dig her heels into the dirt to keep him from bolting after the bird. Excessive movement while on line indicates a lack of steadiness and manageability, and a need for more training.

Bo's response to Sunny's directional commands is extremely important because if Bo doesn't see or doesn't remember where a bird fell, he must rely on Sunny for direction. Otherwise, in a real-life hunting situation the bird would be lost. When responding to a directional signal, Bo should continue in the direction he is sent until he either finds the bird or Sunny whistles him to a stop and signals him in a different direction.

As soon as Bo finds his bird, he should hurry back to Sunny and make the delivery. A delivery is considered good when Bo takes the bird right to Sunny and gives it up easily. Dropping the bird, holding it out of Sunny's reach, or holding it so tightly that Sunny has to pry open his mouth to take it will all lower Bo's trainability score. Good retrievers are known for having gentle mouths so they can carry delicate creatures without damaging the meat. Therefore, a retriever with a mouth so hard that it shatters the bird's bones and makes the meat unfit to eat will not receive a qualifying score.

If Bo has good instincts and a little basic training, he will probably perform his four marks to the satisfaction of the judges. That will earn him a qualifying score—one triumphant "leg" toward his Junior Hunter title.

EVALUATING POINTING BREEDS

The traditional purpose of the pointing breeds is to find game birds and pinpoint their location for the hunter. Bo is eligible to enter hunting tests for the pointing breeds if he is a registered Brittany, Pointer, German Shorthaired Point-er, German Wirehaired Pointer, English Setter, Gordon Setter, Irish Setter, Vizsla, Weimaraner, or Wirehaired Pointing Griffon.

Mikie Moroz, 6, signals Gumbo to line the blind during a training session.

At the Junior Hunter test, Bo and his bracemate (another dog entered in the test at the same level) will break away (be released) and be tested at the same time, so it's important that Bo concentrate on finding game birds and not interfere with his bracemate. Junior level dogs will be allotted at least 15 minutes, and no more than 30 minutes, to complete the test. The dogs may be tested by running a course only, a bird field only, or a combination of both. A bird field is an area of five or more acres where game birds have been placed in natural cover (vegetation, such as bushes or patches of high grass). If a bird field is not used, birds will placed in natural cover on the course.

Every time Bo finds a bird he should go on point (stand absolutely still with his muzzle facing the game bird—with or without a raised foreleg). He will be expected to hold point until Sunny gets within normal gunshot range. If Sunny is within reasonable gun range when the bird is flushed (flies) following a point, she will fire a blank (starter's pistol), to simulate a hunter shooting at the bird. Then she and Bo will continue hunting until time is called. All the handlers will hunt on foot, but Bo should be familiar with horses before attending a test because the judges may be mounted.

TAKING THE TEST (POINTING BREEDS)

At the junior level, pointing breeds are evaluated in four categories. Bo will qualify in the first category, hunting, if he runs a useful pattern, searching the course objectives (areas such as hedgerows or thick cover, where game birds are likely to be found), shows a strong desire to find birds, and has enough independence to cover the amount of ground necessary for a thorough hunt. Teamwork between Bo and Sunny is also important. While independent in his search, Bo should take direction from Sunny, allowing her to select the general direction of the hunt.

Bird-finding ability is the second category, and it means Bo must demonstrate the ability to find game. Birds have been planted (placed) on the course or in the bird field (or both), so a dog that is actually hunting, and not just out for a run in the woods, will find them. Dogs going birdless (failing to find birds) will not qualify.

If Bo points his birds with intensity and confidence and pinpoints their location well, his stylish demeanor will be rewarded with a qualifying score in the third category, pointing. Dogs that appear wishy-washy about whether or not they scented a bird receive low pointing scores.

The final category judged at the Junior Hunter level is trainability (attributes acquired through training, rather than instinct). Its three major components are response to the sound of gunfire, willingness to be handled, and obedience to the handler's commands. Bo will surely qualify in trainability if he responds reasonably to low-key commands and does not resent or ignore Sunny's handling. Hunting tests simulate real-life hunting situations, and lots of screaming in the woods would surely scare off wild game, so if Sunny has to make excessive noise to get his attention, it will lower his score. It's extremely important that Bo shows no fear of the sound of shots. Gun-shy dogs will not qualify at hunting tests because they wouldn't be viable hunting companions.

Performing to the judges' satisfaction in all four categories will give Bo the first leg toward his Junior Hunter title. Advancing to Senior and Master tests will add two new categories: retrieving and honoring. Both are thoroughly explained in the regulation booklet for AKC hunting tests for pointing breeds.

EVALUATING SPANIELS

Spaniels are flushing breeds. Their traditional work is to hunt and find game birds, flush them out of hiding and into the air so the hunter can shoot, and then retrieve them for the hunter. If Bo is a registered Cocker Spaniel, English Springer Spaniel, Welsh Springer Spaniel, Clumber Spaniel, English Cocker Spaniel, Field Spaniel, or Sussex Spaniel, he's eligible to enter spaniel hunting tests.

During the Junior Hunter test, Bo will be tested on land and water. For the Land test, Sunny will have Bo hup (sit) in front of her until the judge tells her to send him. Then he will have approximately 10 minutes to find, flush, and retrieve two birds that have been planted (placed) in natural cover (vegetation). The Water test is a simple water retrieve of a shot bird.

When Lyn Edwards was 11, she and her puppy, Jenny, won first place in a Junior Puppy class. In this photo Lyn is 13, and she and Jenny just earned AKC's highest hunting test title, Master Hunter. Now Lyn has been invited to judge puppy tests.

On the value of participating in this sport, we hear from Pam Edwards of Jackson, Mississippi. "Hunting Tests are very good for young people. They definitely taught Lyn [her daughter] responsibility and that she can do anything through hard work. Lyn has also met several good adult friends who have all helped her tremendously.

"One difficult thing is that after a dog finishes its puppy training, it can't just be trained in the backyard anymore, so parents have to take young trainers somewhere with open ground and water. So, since Lyn has no driver's license, I became her private chauffeur. Larry and I also had to make time commitments to travel with Lyn and Jenny to out of town tests.

"Hunting tests can be very nerve-racking and I did my best to help Lyn keep from getting too nervous or too disappointed if Jenny did not do what she was supposed to. All and all, hunting tests have been very good for Lyn, and I am so glad she has something better to do than walk the mall."

And from Lyn: "I think I have become more patient since I began dog training. I also learned responsibility and commitment. A dog is not a part-time job. It is like your baby, and you always have to know where it is and remember to feed it on time.

"Through the Magnolia Retriever Club I met plenty of people who helped me along the way. I owe everything

I know to them. When I began, I didn't even know how to train a dog to sit.

"Now Jenny is a Master Hunter and I try to train her once a week. When she was younger I had to train her every day."

TAKING THE TEST (SPANIELS)

Bo will be scored in five categories. The first one is hunting ability, and it includes desire, courage, perseverance, and intelligence. Bo will pass this category by hunting with enthusiasm from start to finish, fearlessly checking all cover that might contain birds, and working efficiently for Sunny. The second category, bird-finding ability, includes bird sense, response to wind and scenting conditions, and use of nose. To qualify in this category, Bo should demonstrate an ability to zero in on the type of terrain where birds are generally found, and make intelligent use of the wind direction to help him scent birds. Ultimately, he must find birds. Dogs that go birdless will not pass the test.

The third category is flushing ability, and it's evaluated only during the Land test. Bo will score high in this category if he is fearless and bold about convincing game birds that they simply cannot hide from him and would be better off in the air. A game bird is considered flushed when it flies out of cover. Dogs that find game but are reluctant to get close enough to flush it, will not pass this part of the test.

Bo's trained abilities (attributes acquired through training rather than instinct), will be evaluated in the fourth category. Included are range, pattern, gun response, and response to commands. Bo should work at a reasonable distance from Sunny (not so close as to be inefficient and not so far as to be out of gunshot range). He should also cover ground quickly (for his breed) and effectively, checking all likely cover.

Since hunting tests simulate natural hunting conditions, and too much noise would scare off wild game, Bo should respond to Sunny's low-key signals, whistles, and verbal commands. He should also wait quietly beside Sunny for the signal to retrieve in water. While she may physically restrain him by holding him on lead or by the collar, he should not leap into the air or pull her forward in his zeal to retrieve the bird before being sent. Also, he must show no fear at the sound of a gun.

The final category Bo will be evaluated on is retrieving abilities, and it includes marking, enthusiasm, and mouth. Bo will do fine if he marks (watches and remembers) where his birds fall so he can find and retrieve them easily. His retrieves should be quick and eager, and he should carry his bird gently, without damaging the meat.

HOW AKC HUNTING TESTS ARE SCORED (GENERAL)

Retrieving, pointing breed, and spaniel tests are all scored in the same manner. Two judges evaluate each dog and give it a score ranging from 0 to 10 in each category. Ten is considered perfect, like getting an A+ in school, nine is like earning an A, eight a B, seven a passing grade of C, and so on. Then the individual scores in each category are added together and averaged. To qualify for a leg toward the Junior Hunter title, a dog must earn an overall average of seven for the entire test with no score below five in any single category.

GETTING INVOLVED IN HUNTING TESTS

A good player knows the rules of the game, so before Sunny enters hunting tests, she should read and understand the regulations. AKC rule books also contain pages of regulations for clubs holding hunting tests. Sunny doesn't need to know those right away, but they will help if she ever volunteers to serve on a hunting test committee. Meanwhile, she should study the sections of the regulations dealing with test requirements, performance standards and their explanations, requirements for earning a title, and how dogs are scored.

The ideal way for Sunny and Bo to prepare for hunting tests is to join a club devoted to field work. By attending meetings (which often include educational programs), and by working with other club members at practice sessions, Sunny will learn how to handle Bo in the field and Bo will learn how to combine his natural instincts with his learned skills.

Brianna Iverson, 13, of Humble, Texas, and her English Springer Spaniel, Fergie, competing at their first field trial.

Sometimes clubs also offer hunting test seminars, and these are mighty helpful, especially if Sunny already has some basic knowledge but wants to tune up the fine points. Training books, videos, and magazines abound, and most of them are extremely good, especially in conjunction with training classes. But a book or video without lessons isn't enough. Sunny needs people with field knowledge who will critique her handling and Bo's performance at regular intervals. That way neither of them will unknowingly practice bad habits.

There are hundreds of hunting test programs and clubs across the country. To find the one closest to you, contact the following organizations, which hold tests for Bo's breed. Their addresses are in appendix I.

AKC

The American Kennel Club offers tests at three levels for retrievers, pointing breeds, and spaniels. For information, tell them Bo's breed and request a hunting test rule book, a geographical list of field trial and hunting test clubs, and a sample copy of *The AKC Hunting Test Herald*.

Breed Clubs

Many national clubs for individual breeds (such as the German Short-haired Pointer Club of America) offer their own testing programs, and dogs that pass earn working certificates. To find out what is offered for Bo, look up his breed in AKC's geographical list of field trial and hunting test clubs. Directly under the breed's heading will be the address of the national breed club, and the local breed clubs are listed by state. Write to either the national club or the local club nearest you, and ask if working or field tests are offered and what their requirements are. Some clubs offer their own working-test program as well as the AKC hunting tests summarized earlier.

NAHRA

For retrievers, the North American Hunting Retriever Association (NAHRA) holds field tests and awards the titles Started Hunting Retriever, Working Retriever, Master Hunting Retriever, and Grand Master Hunting Retriever. Request a list of clubs and a rule book.

UKC

The United Kennel Club (UKC) also has a noncompetitive retriever program and qualifies dogs as Hunting Retriever, Hunting Retriever Champion, and Grand Hunting Retriever Champion. Request information on their hunting retriever program and their retriever clubs.

"Training and trialing our springers has given my daughter and I something special that requires us spending a lot of time together," says Bob Iverson of Humble, Texas. "Sometimes it's a long cold day in the rain and sometimes it's a sunny day in Estes Park touring the mountains before a trial. Either way we have good quality time together, and I'm glad that we share a common interest. The only downside to Brianna's trialing dogs is the razzing I get from the other trialers about my daughter outdoing the old man—or maybe that's the upside."

Brianna Iverson and Fergie share a proud moment—a third-place win at the Houston Field Trial.

TIPS FOR ATTENDING A TEST

When packing for a hunting test, Sunny should take water and dog food from home, something to shade Bo, flea and tick spray, a stiff brush or comb (depending upon breed) to remove unwanted vegetation after Bo runs, a towel to dry Bo following the water retrieve (if applicable), a leash, the type of collar specified in the test regulations, and a whistle. Sunny should also have layers of comfortable clothing, well-broken-in all-weather boots, and snacks, in case no food or beverages are available at the test site.

The running order will be posted just before the event begins, and depending on when Bo is scheduled to run, Sunny may have the opportunity to join the gallery (audience) and see other dogs and handlers perform prior to her turn. Before leaving Bo alone, she should make sure he is shaded and comfortable. While watching from the gallery, Sunny must still keep track of the running order. It's her responsibility to have Bo ready when the marshal calls them to the line.

WHEN TO THROW IN THE TOWEL

There are a few faults in sporting dogs that even professional trainers don't want to tackle, and chief among these is gun-shyness. If Bo is terrified at the sound of the gun, chances are he will not get over it no matter how much Sunny works with him. In fact, the situation will be frustrating for Sunny and frightening for Bo. There are many other events where Sunny and Bo can enjoy success, but hunting tests and field trials should be ruled out.

PREVENTING GUN-SHYNESS IN A PUPPY

To save time, money, and energy, it's wise to make sure that Bo isn't gun-shy before beginning field training. Do not simply fire a gun near him to check his reaction, as that could easily make him gun-shy even though he didn't start out that way.

Though seldom correctable, gun-shyness is often preventable. From puppyhood on, Bo should be near a center of human activity, hearing normal household noises such as pots and pans clanking, or a radio playing. Incorporating noise into Bo's feeding schedule is also helpful. This can be done by banging the bottom of a pan while Bo is eating (first gently and from far away, then gradually getting closer and louder day by day). The objective is for Bo to notice the noise but not fear it, then ignore it and continue eating. Creating a lot of clatter while preparing Bo's food may also help him associate noise with a pleasant experience.

Another preventative method that works wonders with six- or seven-week-old puppies may also prove useful with an adult dog that has never experienced gunfire. A family member should hold Bo while Sunny gives him a little taste of his favorite treat from a bowl. After Bo takes a few bites, Sunny should take the bowl and walk 40 or 50 feet away while Bo watches. Then she will fire a blank and return to give Bo the rest of the food. Sunny should repeat this several times over several days, gradually shooting closer, until Bo associates the sound of a gun with a pleasant experience.

Later, she should take Bo to the field and fire a blank pistol as he excitedly begins to find birds. (Firing any gun, even a starter's pistol, shouldn't be taken lightly. An adult who is knowledgeable in gun safety should accompany Sunny). Repetition produces a dog that associates the sound of shots with the pleasure of hunting, one with the potential to succeed at hunting tests.

FIELD TRIALS

Similar to hunting tests, field trials are competitive sporting events for retrievers, spaniels, and pointing breeds. Titles such as Field Champion and Amateur Field Champion are awarded to dogs when they earn the required number of points through defeating other dogs in competition.

Exciting and challenging, but rather advanced for most young trainers, field trials are more suitable for handlers who have already enjoyed some success in the hunting test program. Exceptions are youngsters whose parents are trialers, as they grew up in the sport.

Chapter 16

Lure Coursing

Sighthounds were originally bred for live game coursing, and the sport of chasing game with swift hounds has its roots in antiquity. In fact, murals on four thousand-year-old Egyptian tombs depict sighthound-type dogs in full gallop chasing fleet-footed game.

The objective of lure coursing is to give sighthounds an opportunity to participate in a humane sport that simulates their original purpose. In place of live game, the hounds chase a mechanical lure, with plastic bags as "prey." The mechanical lure is made up of a string run through a set of pulleys and laid out so the plastic bags appear to run and turn with an action similar to live game. Courses range between 600 and 1,000 yards and have a minimum of four turns.

Fourth-grader Jillian Van Vliet (right) "slips" the family's Borzoi at a field trial.

Lure coursing is one of the most beautiful and exciting sports available to dogs, and if Flash is a registered sighthound (a hound bred to hunt wild game by sight and speed rather than by scent) at least one year old, she is eligible to course. Breeds participating in lure coursing include:

Afghan Hounds

Basenjis

Borzois

Greyhounds

Ibizan Hounds

Irish Wolfhounds

Pharaoh Hounds

Rhodesian Ridgebacks

Salukis

Scottish Deerhounds

Whippets

COURSING TITLES

Three different lure coursing titles are available through the American Kennel Club (AKC) and two from the American Sighthound Field Association (ASFA). AKC offers Junior Courser (JC), Senior Courser (SC), and Field Champion (FC), while ASFA offers Field Champion and Lure Courser of Merit (LCM). Sighthounds are judged on speed, agility, endurance, follow (their ability to follow the lure, not cut corners or follow another dog), and overall ability. There are penalties for course delays (for example, a dog that won't let its handler catch it after its run) and preslips (releasing the dog to run before the judge signals the start).

Earning coursing titles takes a moderate amount of commitment. It requires a few minor equipment purchases, attending a few practice sessions, and paying entry fees and traveling (sometimes a considerable distance) to tests and trials. But participating in coursing events is worth the time and effort, and then some. This awe-inspiring sport is made up of exhilarating runs and excellent sportspeople.

THE AKC JUNIOR COURSER TITLE

AKC's Junior Courser title is noncompetitive and is earned by passing a test that evaluates a sighthound's instinct and ability to chase game. When entered in this test, Jerry will walk Flash to the start of the course on a slip lead (a special lead made for quick releases) and release her when the huntmaster cries "tallyho." Flash will run the course alone, and if she completes it with enthusiasm and without interruption (stopping, losing sight of the lure, or running away, for example), she will pass. When she passes two tests under two

Worth the Wait

Anders Yanike, 15, of Union Bridge, Maryland, says coursing has good and bad points, "but the good outweigh the bad many times over.

"I started lure coursing even before I got Fetch," Anders says. "My mother owns a Scottish Deerhound, and she took her to coursing events every month or so. They both loved it, and after hearing so much about it, I decided to go to one.

"As soon as I saw the dogs running in the field, I knew I wanted to get involved. I learned a lot about lure coursing that day. I learned what I didn't like: waiting hours for a familiar dog to run, disgusting dog smells, waiting hours for any dog to run.

"I also learned what I liked: watching a familiar dog run, watching any dog run, relaxing in the car with the radio, eating snacks we got at the nearby 7-11. But what I loved most about lure coursing was the amazing speed of the Greyhounds. The reason I chose Fetch was because of the multi-colored streaks on the field everyone else called Greyhounds.

"Fetch is a retired racing Greyhound with a poor track record. Besides coursing, he loves to lay on beds all day and just relax. He also loves playing with our other dogs, Eddie, a Corgi puppy, and Livvie, a Scottish Deerhound. Lure coursing is exciting and there is a lot to learn about it. One thing I learned is that I will have many sighthounds as my pets in the future."

Anders Yanike and his retired racing Greyhound, Fetch, won Best in Field the very first time they entered lure coursing competition. Anders always slips Fetch himself and carefully cools him down after the course.

different judges, she will receive a Junior Courser certificate from AKC, and the JC title will become an official suffix to her registered name.

ADVANCED TITLES

AKC's advanced titles and ASFA's titles are harder to earn. For example, Flash will have to run with other hounds and must not interfere with them in any way. Three hounds will be slipped at the same time, wearing different colored blankets to help the judges identify them at speed from a distance. While running, Flash will have to show self-confidence and good manners, and chase the lure, not the other hounds. To earn advanced titles, Flash will also have to be a successful competitor, as points toward championships are earned by defeating other hounds. In short, becoming an AKC Field Champion or an ASFA Lure Courser of Merit identifies Flash as a superior courser with ample agility, follow, and speed.

THE HANDLER'S ROLE

Coursing is pure instinct. It isn't something a dog can be trained to do, so Jerry's role in Flash's coursing career will not be trainer. But, if Flash happens to be a natural-born courser, Jerry will have his hands full as both coach and conditioner. He can make the most of Flash's desire by enhancing her ability through good management and careful conditioning.

A coursing career should never be rushed. Dogs with the instinct but not the conditioning can injure themselves on the course, especially when executing abrupt turns. Puppies under six months old shouldn't even try it. So, if Flash is a little puppy, her conditioning should be limited to toys and simple games. Rags and soft stuffed toys encourage puppies to grab, shake, and carry things around, and many people believe puppies with strong grabbing instincts grow up to be the best lure coursers. Dragging a rag and letting little Flash chase it is also productive play, and she should be allowed to catch the rag and play tug with it. But none of these games should be played too long. It's important that Jerry always stop playing before Flash wants to, so she never becomes bored with chasing games.

To prepare for the JC test and beyond, Jerry should begin by taking Flash on long, brisk walks at least three times a week (provided she is eight months or more of age). The walks should build up to two miles, and they will do the most good if Jerry jogs part of the way so that Flash has to trot.

If you have a fenced yard, it can be used for dual conditioning. Flash will build muscles playing alone in the yard; and play between

Jerry and Flash, especially the kind that excites Flash and gets her running, is also helpful.

When conditioning Flash, Jerry should follow commonsense rules, similar to those used by human athletes. Most important are warm-ups and cool-downs. Flash should be walked for half a mile before she is trotted, and cooled down for a half a mile at the end of her workout. She shouldn't be worked at all during dangerous weather, such

Here Jillian Van Vliet waits between races. The Borzoi is wearing a yellow "blanket"; the dogs racing against her will wear different colors.

as very hot, muggy afternoons or days when frostbite or slipping on ice is a possibility. In the summer, she should be worked either early in the morning or during the evening, and if she's worked on pavement, it's important to make sure the concrete isn't hot enough to burn her pads. Also, no matter how diligent a coach Jerry becomes, Flash should have a day off every few days, as muscles need rest periods between exercise.

Flash should be fed a high-quality diet, and fresh water should always be available, especially before and after a workout. However, if she gets very hot during exercise, she should be offered only a small drink of water every few minutes as she cools down.

GETTING STARTED IN COURSING

Before Jerry sets himself up for a possible disappointment, he should discover if Flash was born with the instinct to course. The best way to find out is by attending a coursing club's practice session. Another possibility is going to a coursing trial. At some trials, unentered dogs are allowed to run the course for a small fee after the close of competition.

It's important that Flash runs alone and has a good experience the first time she courses, so make sure the lure operator knows that she is a beginner. After Flash becomes a Junior Courser, she will have to learn to run politely, but competitively, with other dogs. This is best taught by arranging for her to make practice runs with an experienced, stable dog—one that follows the lure no matter what.

To find a coursing club near you, write to the American Kennel Club or the American Sighthound Field Association (appendix I). AKC publishes the *AKC Coursing News* and ASFA publishes the *Field*

Second Family

"I've been going coursing with my mom and dad since I was a baby," says fourth-grader Jillian Van Vliet, of Manchester, Maryland. *A year ago, Jillian's parents surprised her with her own sighthound, a Basenji named Panda. Jillian especially likes watching Panda chase the lure, and says Panda loves doing it. "I also enjoy being with the other dogs and their owners,"* Jillian says. *"Our coursing friends are like my second family."*

Jillian and Panda wait by the lure. Once it is moving, the white garbage bag will simulate a game animal running away, and Panda will chase it at top speed.

Advisory News (appendix 2). Both magazines feature articles on coursing and list coming events.

WHEN THE DREAM IS IMPOSSIBLE

Just because Flash was born a sighthound does not mean she will want to chase a lure. Heredity is extremely important in lure coursing, and if Flash wasn't born with the instinct to chase, nothing will convince her to excel at this sport. So, if Flash shows no interest in the fleeing lure, encourage Jerry to take a look at all the other exciting events they can enjoy together, and choose one of those.

Chapter 17

Herding

If Champ is AKC registered as one of the traditional herding breeds, he's eligible for AKC herding tests and trials. These events preserve and develop the herding skills instinctive to these breeds, and demonstrate that today's dogs can still do the important chores their ancestors were originally bred to perform.

Kelli Herbel, nine, gives Bo, a seven-year-old Australian Cattle Dog, the command to fetch the Blackbelly Barbadoes. Bo is a seasoned ranch and herding trial dog who can work ducks, sheep, goats, cattle, and horses. He has gathered cattle in herds as large as 500. Lori Herbel

While a few of the handlers at herding events actually use their dogs to work stock, the majority are sportspeople who enjoy training their dogs and want to give them an opportunity to use their incredible instincts. Eligible breeds include:

Australian Cattle Dog
Bearded Collie
Belgian Malinois

Belgian Sheepdog

Belgian Tervuren

Border Collie

Bouvier Des Flandres

Briard

Collie

German Shepherd Dog

Old English Sheepdog

Puli

Samoyed

Shetland Sheepdog

Cardigan Welsh Corgi

Pembroke Welsh Corgi

AKC offers herding titles at six levels, from beginner to extremely advanced. Every time Champ earns a qualifying score at a test or trial he will be awarded a ribbon. When he earns a title, he will receive a certificate from the AKC, and the title becomes an official part of his registered name.

HERDING TESTS

Herding tests evaluate a dog's basic instinct and trainability. To be a useful herder, a dog must be capable of moving livestock from one point to another in a controlled manner. That's what is evaluated during the test called the HT (Herding Tested), the first level in AKC's herding program. If Linda enters Champ for the HT, she can expect the following of the test.

When it's Champ's turn to be tested, Linda will walk him into the testing area on leash as the judge watches. If the judge feels that Champ is under control and will not injure the stock, Linda will be told to give a stay command and remove the leash. The test begins when the leash is off, and Champ should remain where Linda left him until she sends him to work the stock.

First, Linda will command Champ to move the stock from the first marker to the second marker, then turn the stock toward the first marker again. Just before they reach the first marker, Champ will have to turn them again and move them toward the second marker. The test ends near the second marker where Linda will give Champ the stop command and call him to her. Throughout the test, Champ must work under Linda's control, while keeping the stock under his control.

Champ will earn a leg toward the HT title if he achieves passing scores on the five required elements: staying in position until Linda releases him; changing the direction of the stock at least twice in a controlled manner (counts as two elements); stopping on command; and coming back to Linda on command (recall). The stock used varies from test to test and might be sheep, ducks, or cattle.

Kelli works Skeet, a 14-month-old Border Collie, on basic maneuvers in a small, round pen. Lori Herbel

The second test level is Pre-Trial (PT). At this level, Champ and Linda will work in a larger area. Champ will earn a qualifying ribbon and a leg toward the title if he remains in position until Linda releases him, successfully collects and controls the stock, puts the stock in motion, moves them both right and left, negotiates several obstacles (this includes clearing four gates and a change of direction), stops on the course on command, stops on command before penning the stock, and pens the stock. Earning a Pre-Trial title means that Champ has the ability and trainability to succeed at competitive herding trials but needs further training to refine his talents.

The first two herding titles are earned by passing two noncompetitive tests under two different judges. Dogs are allowed a maximum of 10 minutes to complete the requirements.

HERDING TRIALS

There are three levels of herding trials and they serve as tests as well as competitions. At each level of difficulty, Champ must qualify three times under three different judges to be awarded a title. Although he is competing against other dogs for placements and awards, he will earn a leg toward a herding trial title every time he obtains a qualifying score, whether or not he wins a placement.

The first trial level is Herding Started (HS), followed by Herding Intermediate (HI), and Herding Advanced (HX). At each higher level, Champ will be required to perform more intricate and controlled work. He will also be expected to think and react independently of Linda's help, while still remaining under her control.

The final, and most prestigious, title of all is Herding Champion (HCh). Before competing for it, Champ must already have the HX title. Then he has to earn 15 championship points by defeating competition in the advanced class. Two first-place wins are required, and one of them has to be in major competition. The number of championship points Champ receives each time he wins or places will depend on the number of dogs entered in competition.

GETTING STARTED IN HERDING

Although Linda may be anxious to start, Champ shouldn't be rushed into herding at too young an age. It's essential that he be capable in three areas before he even sees stock.

First of all, he must have the instinct to herd. Most dogs with the instinct have lots of energy, sometimes run circles around things, are outgoing and confident, and occasionally go so far as nipping at people's heels in an effort to drive them in a certain direction.

Secondly, Champ should be intellectually and emotionally mature enough to use his instinct well. This includes remembering and obeying commands, and learning from each herding experience.

Third, he must be physically mature enough to keep up with the sheep. If Champ still has his puppy clumsiness, he could hurt himself by attempting to handle stock too soon, or become frustrated by his inability to get where his instinct tells him to go. Champ should be no younger than six or seven months old, and meet the requirements above, when he meets stock for the first time.

If Champ's first confrontation with stock doesn't go well, it's no cause for alarm. Many young dogs are given a brief encounter with stock once a month until they show interest and readiness. Having to wait a few months doesn't mean Champ won't be good at herding—only that he isn't ready yet.

Eleven-year-old Lacey Herbel and Ruby, an eight-month-old Border Collie, demonstrate "fetching," which means bringing the stock to the handler. Lori Herbel

Since Champ must be under control in the herding arena, Linda can start preparing for that long before he meets stock. Basic obedience training classes are helpful, and he can start attending them at four months old. A regular novice class, offered by a dog club or a training school, will teach Linda the rudiments of handling Champ while getting Champ used to

In this photo Lacey Herbel sends Skeet on a "come bye," which tells him to go clockwise around the livestock.
Lori Herbel

obeying Linda. But even after Champ is totally reliable on the novice obedience exercises, he may temporarily forget everything he learned during the excitement of seeing stock for the first time. So the first time Champ sees stock, someone with herding expertise should accompany Linda.

Training a herding dog is different from any other type of dog training, and handling well is a challenge in itself, so it's vital that Linda have specialized herding instruction. For example, she'll have to learn to walk backward so she can see the stock while she watches Champ. It's not unusual for new handlers to let their sheep get behind them and then take a couple steps backward and trip over the sheep. Linda also has to learn how to place herself in the best position when Champ is trying to negotiate the stock through an obstacle, such as a gate. If she blocks the gate without realizing it, Champ won't be able to make the stock go in.

It will probably take several weekly lessons before Linda is educated and coordinated enough to train Champ for the HT title and handle him adequately. And if she wants Champ to be competitive at trials, herding lessons could easily continue for two years or more.

FINDING HELP

Getting started in herding doesn't sound easy, does it? Especially not if you live in a city, or even the suburbs, where your neighbors will probably report you to several agencies if you keep ducks or sheep in your yard. But don't worry. If Linda has her heart set on herding, and Champ has enough instinct, they can excel at the sport without owning sheep. In fact, most people who own dogs with AKC herding titles have no farm stock at all.

To start, Linda should read the sections of the regulations that apply to the handler, and attend at least one herding event just to watch. Depending on where you live, finding an instructor may or may not be easy. Start by contacting AKC (appendix 1) to request a list of herding clubs, a booklet of regulations for herding tests and trials, and a geographical list of AKC show and obedience clubs. Check the list of herding clubs first. If there is one near you, it may offer instruction and an opportunity to practice, as well as tests and trials. If not, find your state on the geographical list, then look under "Herding Group" for clubs near you. Contact those clubs whether they specialize in your breed or not, because they may offer training and events for all the herding breeds.

An AKC publication called *The Herdsman*, available by subscription (appendix 2), also lists upcoming tests and trials as well as educational seminars.

BENEFITS OF HERDING

Obviously, herding is a rather heavy commitment. It requires basic obedience training, then specialized training with practice sessions on actual stock, and, finally, transportation and entry fees for events. Is it worth it? What will Linda learn?

A good instructor will teach Linda how to assess the different types of livestock she and Champ will encounter, as well as how to read animal body language. When she learns to appraise the stock's reaction to Champ and his reaction to the stock, she will be able to place Champ at just the right point to maneuver the stock exactly where she wants them. This entails split-second decisions made under the pressure of test or trial conditions, and the situation will never be the same twice. Also, stock is unpredictable, and there will be times when Linda and Champ won't have time to think, only to react.

Training for herding is a slow process where each perfected skill becomes a stepping stone for the next skill, so herding also teaches short-term and long-term goal setting, perseverance, and patience. Bringing out Champ's instinct may take time, but when it emerges, Linda will feel not only satisfaction, but awe. From then on, helping Champ use that instinct productively will be teamwork at its highest level. It will also be healthy, outdoor fun shared with other herding dog handlers.

SISTERS AND STOCKDOGS

Unlike most participants in AKC herding events, 11-year-old Lacey and 9-year-old Kelli Herbel, of Putnam, Oklahoma, are growing up on a working stock ranch. Their father, Kent, is a professional stockdog trainer, and their mother, Lori, is editor of a national herding dog magazine. The girls help out on the ranch, and their everyday chores give meaning and life to the herding dog program.

"Training a stockdog takes a lot of time and patience," says Lacey. "We start them out as puppies, spend lots of time with them, and teach them basic obedience commands. When we start them on livestock, we work them in a small area so we can keep better control of what's happening. It's important to be able to 'read' a dog's body language and work *with* him to encourage his natural instincts, and not 'turn him off' livestock."

Lacey Herbel, 11, and her sister, Kelli, 9, with Skeet, their 14-month-old Border Collie. The girls help with Skeet's training, and he helps them do chores. Lori Herbel

Lacey and Kelli both help their dad train, and Kelli says there are many ways to train a herding dog. "Sometimes we do what we call 'dry work,' which helps the dogs learn herding commands before they actually work livestock. Some of the commands are 'away to me,' which tells the dog to circle the stock counterclockwise; 'go bye,' which means the dog should circle the stock clockwise; and 'that'll do,' which means stop! Once the dogs learn these commands and have some control, we work them on livestock in a round pen so they learn more about herding. After that, they go out in bigger pasture areas.

"My sister and I use dogs every day to help us with chores," Kelli says. "We use them to push and hold the cattle, sheep, and goats away from us while we feed, so they don't push us around and so we have room to put their feed in the feedbunks. We also use our dogs to move livestock from pen to pen. Last spring, my sister and I used two dogs to take 70 head of sheep and goats down the road to graze the ditches. The dogs' job was to keep the animals grazing in the ditches and off the road."

Lacey says she likes herding with dogs because it's fun to work with a dog and not have to do all the work alone. "We work our dogs from horseback when we have to go out in large pastures to check our cattle," she says, "then if a cow needs to be doctored or moved to another pasture, we use the dogs to gather them and put them in a corral."

Trained stockdogs also make it easy to load cattle on a truck. "Just open the trailer gate and let the dogs do the work," Lacey says. "In just a few minutes, the cattle are loaded and ready to go!"

Chapter 18

Earthdog Events

As charming, comical, and spirited as they are, it's no wonder that small terriers and Dachshunds are popular pets. But warming laps and acting adorable were not their original purpose. The small terrier breeds and all varieties of Dachshunds were originally bred to hunt and kill vermin. Their job was to keep farms free of rats, badgers, foxes, and other pests that feed on poultry or contaminate grain. In fact, the word *terrier* comes from the Latin *terra*, meaning "earth" or "ground," and terriers earned their name by going into the ground after their quarry (prey). Today, when few dogs still earn their keep as ratters, earthdog tests and working terrier trials give these feisty breeds an opportunity to prove they inherited the hunting instincts of their ancestors.

These are the breeds eligible for American Kennel Club (AKC) earthdog tests and American Working Terrier Association (AWTA) tests and trials:

Dachshund

Australian Terrier

Bedlington Terrier

Border Terrier

Cairn Terrier

Dandie Dinmont Terrier

Smooth or Wire Fox Terrier

Lakeland Terrier

Norfolk Terrier

Norwich Terrier

Scottish Terrier

Sealyham Terrier

Skye Terrier

Welsh Terrier

West Highland White Terrier

Jeffrey Frier-Murza of Crosswicks, New Jersey, opens the door so his Bedlington Terrier can leave the tunnel after a practice run.

If Pandy is one of these, is registered with the AKC, and is six months of age or older, she is eligible to enter.

AKC'S EARTHDOG TESTS

At AKC tests, dogs enter a tunnel, find their quarry (securely caged laboratory rats), and work the quarry by barking, digging, growling, lunging, or any other action indicating their interest in the quarry. Four noncompetitive tests are offered, each progressively more difficult.

The First Test. The first test is called Introduction to Quarry. It's a simple instinct test that requires no training or experience and does not count toward earning a title. The judge is even permitted to encourage Pandy a little, because it's important that her first exposure to quarry be a positive experience. That makes the introductory test the best place to start, although Chip can skip it if he wants to and enter at the first title level instead.

To begin the Introduction to Quarry test, Chip will bring Pandy to the entrance of the test area on a leash. When it's his turn, he will remove her collar and leash and carry Pandy to the starting marker. Until then, Chip may talk to Pandy and hype her up all he wants. But once he reaches the starting line, he must be quiet and listen to the judge's instructions. Most judges give clear instructions and will make sure Chip understands the test before giving the release command.

When the judge signals the release, Chip will give Pandy one command and release her from waist high or lower. Pandy will go 10 feet to the tunnel entrance, enter the nine-by-nine-inch hole, and make her way through it to the quarry (approximately 10 feet). Since dogs new to the sport usually need a little time to work it all out, the stopwatch doesn't start until Pandy enters the earth. Then she is allowed two minutes to find and begin working the quarry. If Pandy begins

Michael Frier-Murza cheers as his Border Terrier dashes for the practice tunnel. The dog is well on his way to passing the Introduction to Quarry test.

working the caged quarry within the two-minute time limit, and works for thirty seconds without stopping, she will pass her Introduction to Quarry.

The Second Test. Dogs qualifying at the next level, the Junior Earthdog test, earn a leg toward their Junior Earthdog (JE) title. The JE test has two parts, the approach to the quarry and working the quarry. It begins like the Introduction to Quarry test, with Chip giving the release command at the judge's request. After that, it's a little more difficult. Pandy will be timed from the instant she is released, and will pass the first part of the test if she enters the tunnel and reaches the quarry in 30 seconds or less. Once she reaches the quarry, she has a leeway of 30 seconds before she must start working. Pandy will pass the second part of the test if she stays with the quarry until the test is over, works within one foot of the quarry, and continues working for 60 seconds without stopping. When Pandy passes this test twice, under two different judges, she will receive a certificate from the AKC and will be permanently recorded as a Junior Earthdog.

The Third and Fourth Tests. In the wild, animals build complex tunnels, with several entrances and turns, and the width often narrows in areas where there are rocks or large roots. That's why the advanced-level titles, Senior Earthdog (SE) and Master Earthdog (ME), present the dog with a more realistic den situation and involve training as well as instinct.

To earn a Senior Earthdog title, Pandy will have to do more than simply follow the quarry to ground and mark the game (noisily work it) for the handler. She will also have to determine the correct direction taken by the quarry and leave the den on command if the quarry has bolted (left the den). This scenario is simulated during the Senior test by the judge removing the caged quarry from the den (via an above-ground trap door). Although the scent of quarry will still be strong, Pandy will have to prove her manageability as a hunting dog by leaving the den on Chip's command.

Since multiple dogs often hunt together in real life, Pandy will have to prove her ability to work with another dog in order to earn the coveted Master Earthdog title. She will also be expected to decipher the correct den entrance, work her way past a constriction in the tunnel, and continue working the quarry despite distractions overhead.

AMERICAN WORKING TERRIER ASSOCIATION (AWTA) TESTS AND TRIALS

AWTA offers a test on natural ground in an actual hunting situation, as well as competitive trials where artificial earths, similar in design to

AKC's tunnels, are used. At the trials, there are Novice and Open classes. To become eligible for Open competition, a dog has to receive a score of 100 percent in a Novice Class. Scoring 100 percent in an Open Class merits a Certificate of Gameness (CG title). From then on, the dog may compete only in championship trials. Dogs are scored on how quickly they reach the quarry and how enthusiastically they work.

AWTA's highly regarded Working Certificate must be earned in the woods or fields in an actual hunting situation. This includes entering a real tunnel dug by a wild animal that is still in residence, and bolting the animal or holding it at bay for three minutes.

PREPARING FOR TESTS AND TRIALS

Since beginner-level tests and trials evaluate instinct, not training, at first glance it appears that Pandy will either have working ability or she won't, and there isn't much Chip will be able to do about it. It's true that if Pandy shows a driving desire to reach the quarry on her first try, all Chip has to do is enjoy the awesome display of an ancient instinct. But not every Dachshund or terrier is immediately interested in this sport, and it often takes several attempts before the instinct surfaces. There are many reasons why a dog may get off to a slow start. For example, if the dog is reprimanded every time it barks at home, it has to learn that barking is okay in this situation.

Chip can help Pandy get off to a good start by building a simple tunnel and putting it in her play yard. The tunnel should have the regulation nine-by-nine-inch opening, and it only needs three sides (two sides and a top) because it sits on the ground (not underground like the tunnels at actual events). Most home tunnels are built using three-quarter-inch plywood and one-by-ten-foot boards.

Once the tunnel is completed, Chip's most important attribute will be patience. The worst thing he can do is shove Pandy into the tunnel. Instead, he should simply wait. Eventually Pandy's instinct to examine holes will overwhelm her fears and she will check out the tunnel at her own speed.

Chip won't have long to wait if Pandy is a puppy. Puppies love to examine holes and have a strong instinct to enter them. Just providing the tunnel so Pandy can become familiar with it is enough. As Pandy grows bigger, the tunnel won't, and Pandy will gradually get used to going into a more confined area. Later, if Chip wants to, he can add another section or two of tunnel, each at a right angle. This will increase Pandy's readiness for events as well as her fun.

If Pandy is mature when she receives her play tunnel, it will probably take her longer to enter it. Remember, the same opening that looks big to a little puppy, looks small to a grown dog. Pandy may also hesitate because she's already gotten into trouble by putting her nose where it didn't belong, and learned to be cautious about new items in the house and yard. Waiting, not encouragement or training, is the name of the game at this point. The objective is for Pandy to think that going into the tunnel is all her idea.

Some handlers introduce their dogs to quarry at home before taking

Brothers Jeffrey and Michael Frier-Murza work together at giving a young dog a good first experience in the practice tunnel. This gives you an idea of how simple a tunnel is to build.

them to an event, but if the thought of keeping pet rats makes you cringe, rest assured that it isn't necessary. New dogs can learn about quarry during AKC's Introduction to Quarry test or in AWTA's Novice class. Also, AWTA often allows uninitiated dogs to work the earth when the judging is over. But if the idea of pet rats doesn't bother you, and Chip takes good care of his pets, then a couple of domestic rats (available in pet shops) may help awaken Pandy's instinct. Of course, the rats must be kept in a sturdy cage, out of Pandy's reach.

INTRODUCING QUARRY AT HOME

If Pandy is an older puppy (over four months old), she may be introduced to quarry by placing one calm rat on the ground in its sturdy cage. Some of the rat's litter should also be in the cage to enhance the scent. While Pandy checks out the rat, Chip can excitedly repeat the command she will eventually associate with hunting tests and trials, "Rat!" Chip should not be disappointed if Pandy shows little interest at first. Small terriers and Dachshunds were bred for centuries to attack game underground, but young puppies weren't expected to handle the job.

When Pandy does show interest, Chip should resist the temptation to let her work the rat for very long. A minute is more than enough. Also, he shouldn't show her the rat too often or she will soon realize that she can't ever catch it and will become bored. Bringing out the caged rat should be a special occasion, one that occurs once every two weeks for about two months. By then Pandy will be old enough to attend events, and the above-ground initiation should stop. Instead,

Pandy should try working underground at an actual test or at club practice sessions.

If Pandy is an adult when she's introduced to quarry, Chip should use the method described for a puppy but keep one hand on her upper back to give her encouragement and confidence. When she begins to show interest in the rat he could try roughhousing with her, as that excites some dogs into barking. To protect the rat if Pandy begins biting or pushing the cage, Chip should make use of the traditional terrier handle—the dog's tail. The tail hold controls Pandy without making her feel chastised, and is performed by simply holding

Michael gives his terrier a helpful boost out of the tunnel after a successful practice run.

the tail firmly near the base (not pulling). It's important that Pandy not be restrained by the collar, as this may be misinterpreted as a correction for working the quarry. When Pandy becomes so excited by the rat that Chip has to use the tail hold, it's time to stop working above ground and take her to a test or trial.

ATTENDING EVENTS

Because limited breeds participate in earthdog tests and terrier trials, there aren't a whole lot of these events, although their numbers grow annually. The events calendar that comes with the *AKC Gazette* (appendix 2), lists upcoming AKC earthdog tests. For a list of AKC earthdog clubs, where Chip may be able to attend meetings and practices, contact the American Kennel Club (appendix 1).

Write to the American Working Terrier Association (appendix 1) to find out if they have a local club in your area. Their publication for working terrier enthusiasts is called *Down to Earth* (appendix 2), and it lists upcoming trials.

The amount of commitment these tests and trials require depends on the strength of Pandy's instinct and how far Chip wants to go. For example, earning a Junior Earthdog title is a good goal and might be achieved by entering only a few tests. On the other hand, advanced titles involve training as well as instinct, and Chip may have to attend obedience classes with Pandy to achieve the necessary degree of control.

Is it worth it? Many believe it is. Besides meeting fine sportspeople who participate in tests and trials, it's incredibly exciting to see the light go on in Pandy's eyes when she acts out her primeval instincts. Through earthdog events, Chip will gain a deeper understanding of animals, instincts, and heredity than he could ever learn in school.

Part III

STAYING
MOTIVATED

Chapter 19

Making the Fun Last Forever

Dogs aren't like pogs or rock concerts because kids don't always outgrow them. Many of today's animal professionals—veterinarians, research scientists, groomers, technicians, and trainers—discovered their love for dogs when they were kids and pursued their career because of that love. Other dog-crazy kids went into other fields of work but have a beloved dog waiting at home to greet them after a harried day at the office. Some have it both ways. During the week they are doctors, teachers, mechanics, and engineers, and on weekends they take their dogs to field events or shows.

Since awards are available at several levels of expertise, many people are happy with their dog hobby for years as they attempt to achieve ever higher goals. Leadership opportunities await those who excel, and it's not unusual for 4-H kids to grow up and become dog project leaders, obedience competitors to become their club's training instructors, and junior showmanship buffs to become breeders of top winning dogs.

Variety also keeps people coming back, and there is always a new challenge for those who accept it. Obedience competitors add agility to their repertoire, dog show exhibitors try their champions in the field, and many sportspeople enjoy participating in three or more different events with the same dog. In fact, this book didn't even cover every activity available to dog lovers.

OTHER STUFF

There are relay team sports such as flyball and scent hurdles, special shows and hunting events for six coonhound breeds, field trials for Bassets and Beagles, and more. Team sports may be available through your local agility club, and appendix I lists additional events offered through AKC, UKC, and AMBOR.

The kids who enjoy dog events the longest are those who keep them in perspective. Whenever competition is involved, there are moments of incredible elation as well as hours of frustration. Since many dog sports are highly competitive, sometimes kids (and adults, too) need to be reminded why they became involved in the first place. During the down days, try to help your kids remember that before they became obedience competitors or junior handlers, they made dogs part of their life simply because they loved them.

There has always been a special trust between dog and human. Training and participating in activities with a dog enhances that relationship, and frustration should never be allowed to tear it down. When parents put competition in the proper perspective, their kids usually do, too. Someday you may have to remind your child that there will always be another opportunity to compete—but relationships are special.

Appendix 1

Organizations

GENERAL OR MULTI-ACTIVITY ORGANIZATIONS

American Kennel Club (AKC)
51 Madison Avenue
New York, NY 10010
(212) 696-8200

and

5580 Centerview Drive, Suite 200
Raleigh, NC 27606
(919) 233-9780

(Dog shows, junior showmanship, obedience, Canine Good Citizen, tracking, agility, lure coursing, hunting tests, field trials, earthdog tests, herding, and coonhound events)

Also: Geographical lists of dog show and obedience clubs, and hunting test and field trial clubs. Rule books for individual activities. Canine Good Citizen information packets. Use North Carolina address to request written material.

United Kennel Club (UKC)
100 East Kilgore Road
Kalamazoo, MI 49001
(616) 343-9020

(Dog shows, junior showmanship, obedience, agility, hunting retriever program, and coonhound events. Mixed-breed dogs may compete in obedience and agility through affiliations with AMBOR [American Mixed Breed Obedience Registry] and NCDA [National Club of Dog Agility].)

American Mixed Breed Obedience Registry (AMBOR)
205 First Street SW
New Prague, MN 56071
(612) 758-4598

(Obedience, tracking, junior showmanship, agility, Canine Good Citizen, herding instinct, frisbee, versatility, water trials and rescue, flyball, and carting)

SPECIAL ACTIVITIES

4-H

National 4-H Council
7100 Connecticut Avenue
Chevy Chase, MD 20815-4999

(Junior showmanship, obedience, agility, animal-assisted therapy, puppy raiser programs for service dog agencies, animal husbandry, responsibility and leadership training. Activities vary from club to club.)

To locate clubs in your area, call your state Extension Service, listed under "County Government Offices" in your phone book.

Canine Good Citizen

For written material, contact the AKC's North Carolina office. Specific questions can be answered at the New York office. (Both addresses and phone numbers are listed above.)

Obedience

AKC, UKC, and AMBOR (above)
Write to the Superintendents (under Junior Showmanship) to get on their mailing lists.

Animal-Assisted Therapy Volunteer

Delta Society
Pet Partners Program
P.O. Box 1080
Renton, WA 98057
(206) 226-7357

Therapy Dogs International
6 Hilltop Road
Mendham, NJ 07945
(908) 429-0670

Therapy Dogs Incorporated
P.O. Box 2786
Cheyenne, WY 82003
(307) 638-3223

Agility

United States Dog Agility Association (USDAA)
P.O. Box 850955
Richardson, TX 75085-0955
(214) 231-9700

National Club of Dog Agility (NCDA)
401 Bluemont Circle
Manhattan, KS 66502
(913) 537-7022

AKC, UKC, and AMBOR (above)

Tracking

AKC and AMBOR (above)

Puppy Raiser for a Service or Guide Dog Organization

The following groups may need volunteers to help out at their facility
or to serve as puppy raisers :

Guide Dog Programs

Fidelco Guide Dogs
P.O. Box 142
Bloomfield, CT 06002
(203) 243-5200

Guide Dog Foundation for the Blind, Inc.
371 E. Jericho Turnpike
Smithtown, NY 11787
1-800-548-4337 or
(516) 265-2121

Guide Dogs for the Blind, Inc.
P.O. Box 151200
San Rafael, CA 94915
(415) 499-4000

Guide Dogs of America
13445 Glenoaks Boulevard
Sylmar, CA 91342
(818) 362-5834

Guide Dogs of the Desert, Inc.
P.O. Box 1692
Palm Springs, CA 92263
(619) 329-6257

Guiding Eyes for the Blind, Inc.
611 Granite Springs Road
Yorktown Heights, NY 10598
(914) 245-4024

Leader Dogs for the Blind
1039 S. Rochester Road
Rochester, MI 48307
(810) 651-9011

Pilot Dogs, Inc.
625 W. Town Street
Columbus, OH 43215
(614) 221-6367

Seeing Eye Guide Dogs for the Blind
P.O. Box 375
Morristown, NJ 07963
(201) 539-4425

Southeastern Guide Dogs, Inc.
4210 77th Street East
Palmetto, FL 34221
(813) 729-5665

Hearing Dog Programs

Dogs for the Deaf
10175 Wheeler Road
Central Point, OR 97502
(503) 826-9220 voice/TTY

International Hearing Dog, Inc.
5901 E. 89th Avenue
Henderson, CO 80640
(303) 287-3277 voice/TTY

Paws with a Cause
1235 100th Street SE
Byron Center, MI 49315
(616) 698-0688

Assistance Dog Programs

Assistance Dog Institute
P.O. Box 2334
Rohnert Park, CA 94927
(707) 585-0300

Canine Companions for Independence
P.O. Box 446
Santa Rosa, CA 95402
(707) 528-0830

Canine Partners for Life
#130 D, RD 2
Cochranville, PA 19330
(610) 869-4902

Freedom Service Dogs
P.O. Box 150217
Lakewood, CO 80215
(303) 234-9512

Handi-Dogs, Inc.
P.O. Box 12563
Tucson, AZ 85732
(602) 326-3412

Independence Dogs for the Mobility Handicapped
146 State Line Road
Chadds Ford, PA 19317
(215) 358-2723

Junior Showmanship

AKC, UKC, and AMBOR (above)

Mixed Breed Dog Club of California
100 Acacia Avenue
San Bruno, CA 94066
(also offers obedience)

Licensed Superintendents (send them a postcard with your name
and address, and ask to be put on their mailing list to receive premium
lists for dog shows):

William G. Antypas
P.O. Box 7131
Pasadena, CA 91109

Jack Bradshaw
P.O. Box 7303
Los Angeles, CA 90022

Margery Brown
P.O. Box 494665
Redding, CA 96049

Norman E. Brown
P.O. Box 2566
Spokane, WA 99220

Thomas Crowe
P.O. Box 22107
Greensboro, NC 27420

Helen M. Houser
P.O. Box 420
Quakertown, PA 18951

Ace H. Mathews
P.O. Box 86130
Portland, OR 97286-0130

Eileen McNulty
Route 78
Java Center, NY 14082

Jack Onofrio
P.O. Box 25764
Oklahoma City, OK 73125

Bob Peters
P.O. Box 579
Wake Forest, NC 27588

Robert Reed
177 Telegraph Road
Suite 405
Bellingham, WA 98226

Lewis Roberts
P.O. Box 4658
Federal Way, WA 98063

Kevin B. Rogers
P.O. Box 230
Hattiesburg, MS 39403

Elaine Saldivar
4343 Burns Avenue
Los Angeles, CA 90029

Kenneth A. Sleeper
P.O. Box 828
Auburn, IN 46706-0828

Nancy Wilson
8307 E. Camelback Road
Scottsdale, AZ 85251

Kathleen Zimmerman
P.O. Box 6898
Reading, PA 19610

Dog Showing

AKC and UKC (above)
Write to the Superintendents (above) to get on their mailing list.

Hunting Tests

AKC and UKC (above)

North American Hunting Retriever Association (NAHRA)
P.O. Box 1590
Stafford, VA 22555

Lure Coursing

For written material: AKC (above)
To answer questions:

Dean Wright, AKC Coursing Field Director
(717) 637-3011 or (717) 632-6806

American Sighthound Field Association (ASFA)
Kathy Budney
1098 New Britain Avenue
Rocky Hill, CT 06067

Herding

AKC (above)

Earthdog Events

AKC (above)

American Working Terrier Association (AWTA)
Louise Thomas
2580 Town Line Road
Nunda, NY 14517

Appendix 2

Recommended Reading

BOOKS

American Kennel Club. *The Complete Dog Book*. 18th Ed. New York: Howell Book House, 1992.

American Rescue Dog Association. *Search and Rescue Dogs*. New York: Howell Book House, 1991.

Ammen, Amy. *Training in No Time*. New York: Howell Book House, 1995.

Beaman, Arthur. *Lure Coursing*. New York: Howell Book House, 1994.

Benjamin, Carol Lea. *Dog Training for Kids*. New York: Howell Book House, 1988.

Burch, Mary R., Ph.D. *Volunteering With Your Pet*. New York: Howell Book House, 1996.

Fraser, Jacqueline and Amy Ammen. *Dual Ring Dog*. New York: Howell Book House, 1991.

Hall, Lynn. *Dog Showing for Beginners*. New York: Howell Book House, 1994.

Holland, Virgil. *Herding Dogs*. New York: Howell Book House, 1994.

McLennan, Bardi. *Dogs and Kids: Parenting Tips*. New York: Howell Book House, 1993.

Simmons-Moake, Jane. *Agility Training: The Fun Sport for All Dogs*. New York: Howell Book House, 1991.

Spencer, James B. *Hup! Training Flushing Spaniels the American Way*. New York: Howell Book House, 1992.

———. *Point! Training the All-Seasons Birddog.* New York: Howell Book House, 1995.

Volhard, Jack and Wendy. *The Canine Good Citizen.* New York: Howell Book House, 1994.

MAGAZINES

The AKC GAZETTE: The Official Journal for the Sport of Purebred Dogs
The Events Calendar
American Kennel Club
51 Madison Avenue
New York, NY 10010
(919) 233-9767

AMBOR Highlights
The American Mixed Breed Obedience Registration
205 1st Street SW
New Prague, MN 56071
(612) 758-4598

Bloodlines
Rules Special Edition
United Kennel Club
100 East Kilgore Road
Kalamazoo, MI, 49001-5597
(616) 343-9020

Dog Fancy
Fancy Publications
3 Burroughs
Irvine, CA 92718
(714) 855-8822

Dog World
29 N. Wacker Drive
Chicago, IL 60606
(312) 609-4340

RULES & REGULATIONS

Canine Good Citizen

AKC Canine Good Citizen Program Booklet, single copy available free from the American Kennel Club, 5580 Centerview Drive, Suite 200, Raleigh, NC 27606-3390.

Obedience

Obedience Regulations, single copy available free from the American Kennel Club, 5580 Centerview Drive, Suite 200, Raleigh, NC 27606-3390.

Agility

Regulations for Agility Trials, single copy available free from the American Kennel Club, 5580 Centerview Drive, Suite 200, Raleigh, NC 27606–3390 (919) 233-9780.

Tracking

Tracking Regulations, single copy available free from the American Kennel Club, 5580 Centerview Drive, Suite 200, Raleigh, NC 27606-3390.

Junior Showmanship

Junior Showmanship, Regulations, Judging Guidelines and Guidelines for Juniors, single copy available free from the American Kennel Club, 5580 Centerview Drive, Suite 200, Raleigh, NC 27606-3390.

Dog Showing

A Beginner's Guide to Dog Shows, single copy available free from the American Kennel Club, 5580 Centerview Drive, Suite 200, Raleigh, NC 27606-3390.

Rules Applying to Dog Shows, single copy available free from the American Kennel Club, 5580 Centerview Drive, Suite 200, Raleigh, NC 27606-3390.

Hunting Tests

AKC Hunting Test Herald, American Kennel Club, 5580 Centerview Drive, Suite 200, Raleigh, NC 27606-3390 (919) 233-9780.

General Procedures, Regulations and Field Procedures and Judging Guidelines for NAHRA Hunting Retriever Field Tests, North American Hunting Retriever Association, P.O. Box 1590, Stafford, VA 22555.

Regulations and Guidelines for AKC Hunting Tests for Retrievers, single copy available free from the American Kennel Club, 5580 Centerview Drive, Suite 200, Raleigh, NC 27606-3390 (919) 233-9780.

Regulations for AKC Hunting Tests for Pointing Breeds, single copy available free from the American Kennel Club, 5580 Centerview Drive, Suite 200, Raleigh, NC 27606-3390 (919) 233-9780.

Regulations for AKC Hunting Tests for Spaniels and Guidelines for Spaniel Hunting Tests, single copy available free from the American Kennel Club, 5580 Centerview Drive, Suite 200, Raleigh, NC 27606-3390 (919) 233-9780.

Lure Coursing

AKC Coursing News, American Kennel Club, 5580 Centerview Drive, Suite 200, Raleigh, NC 27606-3390 (919) 233-9780.

Field Advisory News, Vicky Clarke, ed., P.O. Box 399, Alpaugh, CA 93201 (209) 949-8649 weekdays, 7 A.M. to 4 P.M. (Pacific Standard Time).

Regulations for Lure Coursing Tests and Trials, single copy available free from the American Kennel Club, 5580 Centerview Drive, Suite 200, Raleigh, NC 27606-3390 (919) 233-9780.

Herding

General Regulations for Herding Tests and Trials, single copy available free from the American Kennel Club, 5580 Centerview Drive, Suite 200, Raleigh, NC 27606-3390 (919) 233-9780.

The Herdsman, Lori Herbel, ed., Route 1, Box 52A, Putnam, OK 73659 (published by AKC).

Earthdog Events

Down to Earth, publication of the American Working Terrier Association (AWTA), Louise Thomas, ed., 2580 Town Line Road, Nunda, NY 14517.

Regulations for Earthdog Tests for Small Terriers and Dachshunds, single copy available free from the American Kennel Club, 5580 Centerview Drive, Suite 200, Raleigh, NC 27606-3390 (919) 233-9780.

Index